Beauty
BEYOND
THE ASHES

Beauty
BEYOND
THE ASHES

Choosing Hope after Crisis

CHERYL MCGUINNESS
WITH LOIS RABEY

HOWARD
PUBLISHING CO.

Our purpose at Howard Publishing is to:

• *Increase faith* in the hearts of growing Christians

• *Inspire holiness* in the lives of believers

• *Instill hope* in the hearts of struggling people everywhere

Because He's coming again!

Beauty Beyond the Ashes © 2004 by Cheryl McGuinness
All rights reserved. Printed in the United States of America
Published by Howard Publishing Co., Inc.
3117 North 7th Street, West Monroe, Louisiana 71291-2227
www.howardpublishing.com
In association with the literary agency of Alive Communications, Inc.
7680 Goddard Street, Suite 200, Colorado Springs, CO 80920

04 05 06 07 08 09 10 11 12 13   10 9 8 7 6 5 4 3 2 1

Edited by Michele Buckingham
Cover design by LinDee Loveland
Interior design by Gabe Cardinale
Cover photograph of Cheryl and children by Bobbi Slavin, Timeless Art Portraits

McGuinness, Cheryl, 1961-
    Beauty beyond the ashes : choosing hope after crisis / Cheryl McGuinness with Lois Rabey.
        p. cm.
    ISBN 1-58229-389-9
    1. Consolation. 2. McGuinness, Cheryl, 1961-3. McGuinness, Thomas F., d. 2001. 4.
September 11 Terrorist Attacks, 2001—Religious aspects—Christianity. I. Rabey, Lois
Mowday. II. Title.

BV4905.3.M348 2004
248.8'66'0924—dc22
[B]
                                                                    2004047533

Scripture taken from the HOLY BIBLE, NEW INTERNATIONAL VERSION®. Copyright ©
1973, 1978, 1984 by International Bible Society. Used by permission of Zondervan. All rights
reserved.

Photo credits: Jackets with caps; *The Boston Globe*; September 26, 2001; *Globe* Staff
Photo/Suzanne Kreiter. Used with permission. Cheryl and Tommy at podium; *Foster's Daily
Democrat*; September 17, 2001; AP Photo/Rich Beauchresne. Used with permission. Jennifer
singing; *Foster's Daily Democrat*; AP Photo/Jess Richardson. Used with permission. Cheryl and
children receiving flag; *San Diego Union Tribune*; AP Photo. Used with permission. Cheryl speak-
ing; *Foster's Daily Democrat*; September 12, 2002; Photo by Aaron Rhode, reprinted courtesy of
Foster's Daily Democrat. Used with permission. Cheryl and children praying; *The Fallbrook/Bonsall
Village News*; October 11, 2001; AP Photo/Ron Jonason. Used with permission. Cheryl giving her
book to President Bush; *The Union Leader*; March 26, 2004; *The Union Leader*/Bob LaPree;
Manchester, N.H. Used with permission.

To my Lord and Savior, Jesus Christ,

who gave me life and a new dream.

To Tom McGuinness,

my husband, my best friend, my soul mate.

Your living testimony was an example for us all.

To our children, Jennifer and Tommy. I love you.

Contents

Acknowledgments

With special thanks:

To my children, Jennifer and Tommy, for your love, support, and encouragement. You make my heart smile, and you bless my life in so many ways.

To Pastor Larry and Annie Grine, for being faithful servants and leading Tom to Christ. Thanks to our Riverview Church family for taking care of us all the way from the West Coast.

To Toby and Carol Stowe, for sharing your time and gifts in helping me wrap words around my thoughts. Also, for supporting my new dream: Beauty Beyond the Ashes ministry.

The children and I quickly realized that everything about the way we lived our lives was now subject to change: *He isn't coming home. Life will never be the same again.*

Introduction

The Day My World Fell Apart

As Tom leaned over the bed to kiss me good-bye, I reached up and sleepily wrapped my arms around his neck.

"Have a good trip," I whispered.

"I'll call you tonight," he said with a smile.

It was the morning of September 11, 2001—a morning like hundreds of other mornings in our eighteen years of marriage. As a copilot with American Airlines, Tom routinely got up in the predawn hours on the days he was flying and kissed me good-bye before heading off to work.

A few hours later, I crawled out of bed as usual, drove the kids to school, then returned home and settled down in a lawn chair on our backyard deck. The late summer day in our hometown of Portsmouth, New Hampshire, was brisk and already beautiful. The trees surrounding our house cradled the deck in quiet peacefulness, and rays of sunlight peeked through the branches, giving the promise of a sunny day ahead. I wrapped a quilt around me and opened my Bible.

Just as I finished praying, the phone rang.

"Cheryl, is Tom home?" asked Chris, one of our good friends.

"No, he left this morning on a trip."

The other phone line started ringing. I put Chris on hold and answered the second call.

It was Bob, another good friend.

"Cheryl, is Tom home?"

I went back and forth between Chris and Bob for a few minutes, trying to understand why both men sounded so anxious yet weren't saying anything specific.

"Do you have the television on?" one of them asked.

"No, I don't watch television in the morning."

The silence on the line was deafening.

My hand shaking, I grabbed the remote and waved it toward the television. "What's going on, Chris?" I cried into the phone.

"A plane has been hijacked, Cheryl. I'm coming right over."

As I stared at the confusing images on the television screen, I tried to reach Tom on his pager and cell phone. I didn't know where he was flying that day, but not knowing was normal. He traveled so much, to so many places. He always called from his cell phone later in the day, and I'd hear all the details of his trip.

Where was he now? I was sure I could find out just by calling him.

I dialed his cell phone again.

No answer.

I was nervous but not panicked. After all, dozens of flights had left Boston that morning. Tom could have been on any of a number of them. Surely he had nothing to do with the nightmare that was unfolding on the television screen.

I tried the number again. Still no answer. *He always answers his cell phone*, I thought.

My apprehension rising, I called a few other American Airlines pilots to see if they knew what flight Tom was on. No one would give me a concrete answer. I had never called American's emergency crew-tracking number before, but now I looked up the number and dialed it. When I finally got through, the airline personnel wouldn't tell me anything over the phone.

My calm September morning was rapidly erupting in chaos.

People began showing up at the house with concerned looks on their faces. Several women came up to me, took my hands in theirs, and began praying. Our kids, Jennifer and Tommy, ages sixteen and fourteen, called from school wanting to know if Dad was OK.

Then our pastor walked in.

This is really bad, I thought.

"Why are you here, Fred?" I asked him.

Before he could answer, I saw the car.

I knew immediately what it meant. After all, I had been a navy wife for years. As the big black car pulled up at the end of our driveway and three or four men in dark suits got out, followed by a priest, I suddenly understood why I hadn't been able to get any information over the phone.

They don't call. They come. The men in the big black car come to the door. They look grim, and you see their ties moving in and out as deep breaths prepare them for the words they will have to utter. They are silent as they move closer to the door, their footsteps echoing off the cold concrete.

It could have been a scene in a movie—but it was my life. I was center stage. I was the waiting wife of the man who would never come home again.

"No, no, no, God! Please don't call him home!" I screamed. I beat on Fred's chest as I cried out the same words again and again. Fred just held me. Finally I stopped and sank into his arms.

I knew that one of the men who had gotten out of the black car must be the chief pilot for American Airlines—the one whose job it was to make this kind of call, the one who had the ominous duty of personally informing family members of the death of a loved one.

I looked up at him now. "Do you have something official to say to me?" I asked.

I saw the pain in his face as he told me that American Airlines Flight 11 had been hijacked and crashed into the World Trade Center in New York City. There were no sur-vivors. Tom had been the copilot on that flight.

Shock overwhelmed every nerve in my body. I felt as if my heart had been ripped out. Nothing seemed real—and yet everything was so real. I gripped Fred's arms to keep from col-lapsing.

It had been such a beautiful morning, such a normal day. I had opened my Bible and then . . . *Tom was gone.* How could this be? Through my shaking and tears, I could see many of my close friends standing around me. They were in the entryway of the house, spilling over into the family room, the dining room. No one said a word. But their faces revealed the compassion and sorrow each one felt for me and my children.

Just when I thought I couldn't feel pain any deeper, I realized that I had to tell Jennifer and Tommy what had happened. I had to give them the news that would do to them what it was now doing to me. How could I do that? What words could I say?

Our good friends Jeff and Vickie drove me to the school. I

don't remember the drive. I just remember walking into the principal's office and seeing our church youth pastor already there. Jeff had called ahead to the school to tell them the news and to let them know I was on my way.

Tommy came running into the office, a look of abject fear on his face. I pulled him into my arms and said, "Jesus has called Daddy home." Jennifer came in a moment later, and I repeated the same words to her. There I stood—a grieving mother delivering terrifying, heartbreaking news to her frightened children. We clung to each other and cried.

I reassured them that we would be okay and told them, "Daddy's okay because he's in heaven with Jesus." I believed my words, but I couldn't quite comprehend the reality of them. At that moment the pain was all consuming. Thinking of Tom being with Jesus was comforting. But how would we survive without him? I didn't have a clue.

The ride back home was quiet. I sat between Jennifer and Tommy in the backseat, legs touching, hands held tight. We leaned on each other. We hugged. They both looked scared, and I admit I was too. My mind kept flipping back and forth between the comforting thought of Tom in heaven and the unsettling thought of the children and me on earth without him. I noticed Jennifer and Tommy occasionally peeking over at me and then looking straight ahead, as if trying to read my thoughts so they could digest them for themselves. I knew my response would be the barometer they would use to measure how safe we really were now that our husband, our father, our human protector was gone.

A Flood of Concern

When we got back to the house, people were everywhere. The phone was ringing off the hook, the media were outside the door, food was arriving, flowers were being delivered. Our youth pastor was there with some of the kids from church. He hugged Jennifer and Tommy and stayed right by them in the hours that followed. Our back deck was full of teenagers from school, church, and the neighborhood. It became their gathering spot in a house teeming with people and activity.

My kitchen was full of women taking care of the cooking, making meal delivery charts, and distributing food to the growing crowd that continued to arrive all day. The family room buzzed with muted conversations as people watched the unfolding events of 9/11 on the television. Friends manned the phone in shifts and recorded the calls in a phone log.

Many of the big media organizations called—*Oprah*, *Time*, *CNN*, *Good Morning America*—but I didn't talk to any of them. I couldn't imagine why anyone would want to talk with me. I couldn't bring myself to think about anything beyond the reality of Tom's absence.

I crept up to my bedroom to make a few calls to family members. Tom's mother answered the phone and said she had been trying to reach American Airlines. I confirmed her worst fears and heard the desperate cry of a mother receiving the news that her son was dead.

I called my sister Patty in Nevada. She, too, had heard the news and feared that the hijacked American flight was Tom's.

"I'll come right away and stay as long as you need me," she said.

Other family members also heard the news in shocked disbelief. My sisters Ginny and Linda arrived at the house about the same time that Tom's parents and his sister, Cathy, arrived. The scene they encountered was overwhelming. There were so many people bustling around! I felt devastated all over again seeing Tom's parents sitting on the sofa in the middle of the family room, looking so stunned and lost.

As I moved through the whirlwind swirling around me, my mind drifted back to a conversation Tom and I had had not long before, when we'd gone out to dinner to celebrate our eighteenth wedding anniversary. He'd told me a tragic story about a navy friend of his whose wife was killed instantly in a car accident.

I couldn't imagine such a loss. "I couldn't live here without you," I'd told Tom through tears. "I just couldn't do it."

"If anything ever happens to me, you have to trust God," Tom had responded with a gentle smile. "God will get you through it. Just surround yourself with loving people. People who know Christ. People who will surround you in Christlike love."

Little did either of us know that I would soon be living through what I feared most.

I do trust you, God, and I will trust you, I prayed silently, realizing that I was already surrounded by loving people. My house was full. Every need was being taken care of. People from the school, our church, the airline, and the neighborhood were there. A sense of gratitude seeped into my aching heart, helping to calm my fears.

That night as I tucked my children into bed, we held each other and cried. The pain was excruciating.

"Will we be okay?" they kept asking me over and over. I assured them that we would be, even as I prayed silently that I was telling them the truth.

Finally I went to my own room and lay down. It was the first time I had been alone since early that morning. I hugged my pillow and sobbed. In my anguish I sensed God whispering to my spirit, "I am with you and your children." I cried and cried, begging God to keep Jennifer and Tommy close to him. I was so afraid that this loss would cause them to turn away from their faith. Over and over again I cried out, "God, help us!" Those three words dominated my vocabulary for days.

I must have finally fallen asleep, because I was awakened the next morning by the sounds of people banging and clanging around in my kitchen. I had given my door key to a neighbor and told her to come in whenever she wanted. She had let in a crew of women who were already organizing all the food, flowers, and notes that were beginning to arrive.

One of the associate pastors from our church, Pastor Dave, came over to talk with me about Tom's memorial service. Dave had been a pastor at a church we had attended in California. Now he pastored at Bethany Church, our new church home in New Hampshire. Our two families had arrived in Portsmouth around the same time the year before. The fact that Dave had known Tom and me longer than anyone else in the area was a comfort as we sat down to make the plans for the memorial.

I was determined to set a celebratory tone. Years earlier my own father's funeral had been terribly painful for me. I didn't want my children to have the same kind of experience. Besides, Tom knew Jesus. He was in heaven with his Savior. We had great hope and reason to celebrate.

"I want the service to be a celebration of life," I told Dave. "A celebration of Tom's life and the life that Jesus offers all of us who believe in him."

The next few days seemed to blur into one another. Our

house continued to be full of people, and the help we received amazed me. As I dealt with my grief and made plans for the memorial service, friends, neighbors, and members of our church family took care of all the details of life. Someone did the laundry, the kitchen ran like a well-oiled machine, the phone was always manned and the log regularly updated, and my children were watched over and loved at all times.

We had been in Portsmouth only a year. Surely it should have taken longer to develop enough close relationships to receive such an outpouring of support! But amazingly, the community rallied around us as if we had been with them for decades.

Celebrating Life

The day before the memorial service, my sisters took me shopping to find a dress to wear. I had lost ten pounds in six days, and nothing in my closet fit well.

"I won't wear black," I told them. "It's too sad, and this is a celebration of Tom's life."

In store after store, my sisters pulled dozens of dresses off the racks for me to try on. I went through the motions in a mental fog. *I'm getting a dress for my husband's memorial service,* I kept thinking. It seemed so surreal.

With every black dress they brought to me, I protested. "I'm not happy about Tom being gone, but I *am* happy about him being in heaven. I want that to be the emphasis of the service. I don't want to look sad," I repeated.

In the end, however, I went home with a new black dress. My sisters convinced me that the style was good, and it needed no alterations. "Just get it," they said.

So I wore black to the memorial service. But the tone of the day was anything but black. The children and I missed Tom. We suffered deeply from the pain of losing him. But God comforted our hearts as we prepared to join our friends and family at the church.

Several of Jennifer's and Tommy's friends rode with us in the limousine to the service. Along the way we sang praise songs at the top of our voices and worshiped the Lord with gusto. I thought my heart would burst as I looked and saw my children smiling.

When we arrived at the church, we noticed that the parking lot was full to overflowing. We stayed in the car for a few minutes and prayed for the strength and courage to face what was about to take place. "God help us," I repeated again. A Scripture verse came to my mind: "Where, O death, is your victory? Where, O death, is your sting?" (1 Corinthians 15:55). How amazing it was to experience the presence and comfort of the Lord in such a powerful way at that moment!

Stepping out of the limousine, we walked into a sanctuary filled with light, people, and an almost palpable sense of the presence of God. As we were escorted to the front row, we were more determined than ever to celebrate Tom's life and God's provision of heaven.

During the service Tommy and I both spoke about Tom, and Tommy read some thoughts Jennifer had written about her dad. Gazing out over the sea of faces, I was shocked to realize that I was actually standing and speaking in front of so many people. Church friends, neighbors, family, American Airline's associates, navy buddies who had flown with Tom, government officials, and many other people I didn't even know filled the church. I was nervous, but my desire to communicate our faith overrode my nervousness.

I shared with the audience that the night before Tom died, he and I had talked about our love and faith in God. I had told Tom how much I'd seen God change, shape, and mold him. I'd told him how excited I was about the great work the Creator had done in him, and how much I looked forward to sharing this life and the next with him. Looking back, I felt thankful that God had given me the opportunity to express my feelings of love and affection to Tom so clearly.

At the end of the service, I told the audience that anyone who wanted to take home one of the Bibles from the pews was welcome to do so. About four hundred Bibles were taken that day. (Sometime later, Zondervan Publishing House and the Willow Creek Association donated four hundred Bibles in Tom's memory to Bethany Church to replace the ones that had been removed. The dedication in the front of each Bible reads, "A gift to Bethany Church in memory of Thomas F. McGuinness, Jr., your brother in Christ whose life was marked by his love of God's Word.")

I still hear stories about people who were deeply touched at the memorial service. Every Sunday at church and regularly as I speak throughout the country, people tell me how much Tom's life impacted them, either directly or from hearing about him at the service. Their conversations give me great encouragement and strength. So does the thought that some of those people who took Bibles home with them have a better understanding now of who Jesus is and what he offers them in this life and in the life to come.

After the service the church had a reception, and I had an opportunity to greet many of the people who had come to the memorial. The numbers were overwhelming, but everyone I met was warm and consoling.

By the time the children and I got back to the house, it was aglow with a warmth of its own. A number of women had gone ahead of us and prepared a beautiful buffet. Family, friends, and neighbors were already arriving. The setting reminded me of an old Irish wake. Praise music played in the background, food was put out in abundance, and Tom's navy buddies sat with a circle of people around them as they reminisced about Tom and the good old days. As a navy pilot, Tom had been deployed for months at a time, flying F-14s off aircraft carriers. These men who now spun their tales had spent many long weeks with Tom during those deployments. Their stories seemed to bring something of Tom's positive, can-do spirit into that room of rapt listeners. And with each minute, each hour that passed, I thought, *We are getting through this. One step at a time, we are doing it. We are surviving.*

My sister Patty arrived from Nevada and stayed with us for three weeks. She did everything—cleaned, cooked, wrote notes, took care of Tommy's and Jennifer's needs. (After a while we started calling her Nanny, because she reminded us of Fran Drescher's character on the TV show, *The Nanny*.) Patty's upbeat personality and boundless energy were just what we needed during those first few days and weeks of transition, as we moved from throbbing shock and pain to acceptance of our new life.

The children and I quickly realized that everything about the way we lived our lives was now subject to change. Each day brought a new realization of just that: *Dad's not here. He isn't coming home. We aren't going to be with him . . . not here on earth anyway. Life will never be the same again.* Those were difficult days, but Patty's presence helped to soften their harshness.

At some point Jennifer, Tommy, and I came up with the idea of planting a "tree of life" in our backyard as a personal, living memorial to Tom that we would be able to enjoy for years to come. We chose a beautiful Crimson King Norway maple tree, set it in the ground in just the right spot, and planted four smaller plants around it. We named the four plants I Love You, Forget Me Not, Sweetheart, and Little Buddy. To us, they represent new life. In the future we may add other touches to this special place.

Learning through Loss

It took me a long time to absorb the broader impact of the 9/11 tragedy. In those early weeks and months, I was consumed with my own grief and concern for my children. Life was so different from anything I had ever experienced before. It took all of my energy to focus on being the new head of our household.

I didn't watch television. I'd catch the news only as I overheard people talking. All I knew for sure was that my husband had been killed, and now my country was at war. Only very slowly did I come to realize that Tom was an integral part of an international event that had devastating ramifications for thousands of people in the United States and around the world.

Many spiritual questions surfaced as I tried to grasp where God was on 9/11. Why did this devastation occur? Why did God allow this personal tragedy? But trying to make sense of it all was too much for me. I quickly realized that all I could do was focus on caring for Jennifer and Tommy. All I could do was trust God.

That's still where I am today: trusting God. I am learning so much through this grief process and the experience of living a life I never anticipated. As I reflect back over all the years of my life, I can see that God was, in fact, working in unseen ways in my life long before I even knew much about him. He was preparing me for this road I'm now walking.

Since 9/11 I've had opportunities to speak to thousands of people individually and in groups of all sizes. Initially, the main interest of my audiences was the September tragedy. Since my family was affected in such a close and personal way by the ter-rorist attacks, people wanted to hear what I had to say about that tragic day.

But as I have shared more and more about God's influence in my life before and after 9/11—how God wooed Tom and me, how he changed us both individually and as a couple, how we struggled to live for him in the midst of a fast-track lifestyle, and how my children and I have grown ever closer to God since Tom's death—people have wanted to hear more. They're intrigued with the part Tom's untimely death played in my story, but they are also interested in God's influence and involvement in my life from my earliest days to the present moment.

Admittedly, some of the particulars of my story are uniquely dramatic. But my emotions are universal. I'm really just like you. We all hurt and love, cry and laugh, and long for answers to the deep questions of life: Why are we here? Why does evil happen? What do we do when life unfolds in surprising ways? Where is God in the difficult times?

All of us suffered on September 11, 2001. My story is a very public one, but you have a story too. Thousands of people lost loved ones that day. People all over the world, and especially in the United States, experienced various levels of shock and pain. We endured a universal tragedy that pierced each of our lives in some degree.

Now we live in the aftermath of that day. Our lives are played out against the backdrop of a country familiar with terror. And the anxiety that this backdrop produces is integrally entwined in the comings and goings of our everyday lives.

But God is still alive. He still cares about the smallest detail of our lives. He still wants us to know him and to see his loving hand at work in our hearts and in our homes.

In the pages that follow, I want to share with you my story. I also want to share with you the principles that have guided me at every stage of my life. Each chapter will tell part of the story of my life and of Tom's life too. From our early childhoods to the events of 9/11 and beyond, you'll read about the journey we traveled and how God's principles, spelled out in the Bible, changed us along the way. Since the catastrophe these same principles have continued to shape my life and the lives of Jennifer and Tommy.

The first part of each chapter will tell my story, and the second part will discuss the biblical principle involved so you can apply it to your own life. Our lives are the individual canvases upon which God reveals himself. But no matter how different our pictures may seem, they are all painted with the same brush. The same principles that apply to me apply to you too.

It is my prayer that as you read my story you will see yourself. Your details will be different and unique, but we have so much of the human experience in common: pain, sorrow, fear, confusion. We also have the same ability to enjoy the benefits of a relationship with God: joy, peace, comfort, guidance.

It is also my prayer that you will see Jesus in the pages of this book and that, if you don't know him now, you will come to know him by the time you finish reading. If you already know

Jesus, I pray that these pages will help you draw closer to him and trust him more fully.

As I've learned—and as I'm still learning—with Jesus there is always a way through even the most difficult circumstances. I pray that through the illustration of my life and the application of these few basic principles from God's Word, you will come to know God better, see his hand at work more clearly, and learn how, with God's help, you can overcome any and every challenge that comes your way.

I tingled all the way down to my toes with the wonderful knowledge that Tom and I were meant for each other.

Chapter One

SIMILAR BEGINNINGS

Principle 1
GOD'S PLAN FOR YOU BEGAN TO TAKE SHAPE
BEFORE YOU WERE BORN.

Both Tom and I were blessed to be born into loving families who lived according to religious principles. Many of those principles had been handed down through generations by ancestors who immigrated to the United States from Ireland and Italy. In both our homes, religious faith was more unspoken than overt. It was simply woven into the everyday fabric of our lives.

I was the third of four girls born into the Solferino family. My father owned a heating and air-conditioning business; my mom was a homemaker who sometimes helped Dad out at work.

As good Italian Catholics, my parents made sure we went to

church every Sunday. And since we had one-and-a-half baths in our home, our frantic preparations always began well before the church bells chimed. My dad would get up around 5:00 A.M. to take a shower before the five females in his household began demanding bathroom time. We actually had to schedule our turns in the bathroom. If one of us got pokey and jammed up the traffic flow, the other females would start pounding on the bathroom door and make loud and frustrated entreaties: "Hurry up!" Each of us wanted to walk into church with perfect makeup and not a hair out of place.

Somehow we managed to make it on time most Sundays. I never rebelled against going to church, although I do remember thinking the services were boring. The rituals seemed confusing at times and not particularly meaningful.

I began having spiritual questions at a young age. As a good Catholic, I took my first Holy Communion, was confirmed, and practiced the traditions of the church. But my questions never seemed to get answered. I was spiritually hungry, but I wasn't being fed.

Tom's experience growing up was similar to mine. We were even born in the same hospital and attended the same church! Yet our paths never crossed until much later.

Tom's ancestry was Irish. His father owned his own business as a manufacturer's representative for an electronics company, and his mom was a homemaker. They, too, practiced their Catholic religion with a consistency that influenced Tom to become a moral young man. He played sports, got good grades, respected God, and loved his family. He was the all-American boy.

Accepting Christ

When I was thirteen years old, my girlfriend Pam invited me to go to a Christian summer camp with her. My parents gave their approval, and Pam and I could hardly wait. *What should we pack? Who will be there? Will there be any cute boys?* At thirteen we thought boys were a big deal, even though our romantic experience with them was limited to our fantasies. We were at an age of innocence and wonder, and camp seemed like the perfect place to have some kind of harmless adventure with members of the opposite sex.

Camp Berea was beautiful. It was situated on Newfound Lake in a wooded area of New Hampshire, with acres of unspoiled land just begging young people to run and play and experience God's wonder. I was thrilled with everything about the camp: the scenery, the activities, being with Pam, being on my own away from home.

One day, during a lull in camp activities, I found myself sitting on the steps of our cabin, talking with one of the lifeguards. He was about twenty years old and gorgeous. Pam and I had spotted him the first night, when we were introduced to the camp counselors. His name was Paul, and I had a bit of a crush on him—knowing, of course, that it would never be more than one sided. I have to admit, there was a certain safety in feeling giddy about someone and, at the same time, knowing that those pleasant stirrings would never be complicated by any real action.

It was raining, and Paul had seen me sitting on the steps with my arms wrapped around my shoulders, trying to warm up. He sat down and started talking. At first I was nervous—*What if I say something stupid?*—but he quickly put me at ease with his warm manner and totally appropriate behavior. Soon my girlish awe of him was forgotten, and I listened to his words with rapt attention.

He was talking to me about Jesus. Nothing he said seemed unusual at first. After all, I had been in church all of my life. But then he began to talk about having a personal relationship with Jesus—about inviting Jesus into your heart and making a conscious decision to be a Christian.

"Do you know for sure that you would go to heaven if Jesus came back this very moment?" he asked.

I wasn't sure. But I wanted to be.

Paul and I talked for a long time, and I prayed to accept Christ that rainy day at Camp Berea. Immediately I felt a warmth inside that gave me an assurance I had never experienced before. That night around the campfire, we sang praise songs, and tears of sheer joy spilled down my face.

When I went home, I told my father what happened, but he didn't understand. My Italian Catholic family didn't express their faith the same way the people at the camp did. I didn't judge them, but I knew I had encountered God in a different way—a deep, fresh way that was unlike anything I had known growing up.

For weeks afterward I'd go up to my bedroom, close the door, and sing the camp songs I'd learned. I'd read the Bible my friends at camp gave me and try to keep the blush of first love with Jesus alive. Over the next few years, though, my passion dwindled. I still loved Jesus and had assurance of my salvation, but my faith wasn't nurtured. I wasn't in an environment conducive to spiritual growth.

High-School Days

My high-school days were pleasant. I was shy and quiet, but I had some close friends, and I loved being involved in athletics. I ran cross-country and track and got satisfaction from the discipline required to excel in those sports. Sometimes my older sisters, Ginny and Patty, called me goody two shoes, but their name calling didn't really bother me. They teased me, too, about being skinny. They weren't meanspirited—just teenagers being older sisters.

Besides, I think my relationship with my mother countered any potentially harmful effects. My mom was my best friend. We hung out together, went shopping, and went out to lunch with my grandmother. I even liked to help Mom clean the house. The close bond between us nurtured my self-esteem and gave me a quiet confidence in myself.

Then Tom McGuinness came into my life. It wasn't exactly love at first sight, but I was definitely struck right away by his good looks. He was drop-dead gorgeous: tall, dark hair, blue eyes, and a smile that beamed when he talked.

He was a senior, and I was a sophomore. I often saw him in the halls of the school and in the cafeteria. I also sat next to Tom's sister, Cathy, in typing class. She encouraged her brother to ask me to his prom, but Tom was shy. Besides, he wasn't about to have his sister tell him what to do.

We finally met in a rather ordinary way. I loved to sew, and I would often spend some of my lunch hour in the sewing classroom working on projects. I'd make a pantsuit with a matching hat or work on some other intricately designed pattern. (I even won a sewing award!) One day Tom and some of his friends came into the sewing room and started to talk and joke around. It was comfortable, easy, and fun. Many times after that, I'd be sewing, and Tom would come in, sit down next to me, and talk away.

Two days before his senior prom, he invited me to be his date. I was surprised and not sure how to answer at first. I didn't know why he had waited so long to ask me, and I'd just gone to another prom with someone else. Conflicting thoughts ran rapidly through my mind. Of course I wanted to go, but I didn't want to get a reputation as an easy date, given the late notice and my other recent prom invitation. Besides, I didn't have a dress to wear, because I couldn't wear the one I'd just worn to the other prom.

"I'll have to ask my mom," I finally said.

Well, my mom gave her permission. I decided to risk my reputation, and I borrowed a dress from my sister: a golden yellow, floor-length gown that my grandmother had made, with handsewn beads on the bodice. I completed the outfit with strappy, high-heeled sandals and long, beaded earrings that matched the beading on the dress.

Tom and I picked out his tuxedo together the day before the prom: cream-colored with a yellow ruffled shirt and a chocolate-colored bow tie. A matching chocolate-colored stripe ran down the outside of each pant leg. Black patent-leather dress shoes and a yellow boutonniere were the finishing touches.

I remember that after we got the tux, we stopped at a

restaurant for a casual dinner. Tom ordered a hamburger and a glass of milk. Now, ordering a Coke would have been OK, but milk? That wasn't considered cool! But Tom was comfortable enough with himself to order what he wanted. It seemed like such a small thing, and yet it revealed a tiny speck of Tom's character that I really liked. He wasn't trying to impress me or anyone else. He was just being real.

After the prom and Tom's graduation, we continued to see each other all summer. We'd talk for hours about so many different things. Tom even taught me to drive. And even though we hadn't run into each other much in church before, we now found that church provided another way for us to be together. We decided to team-teach a Sunday school class. The church provided a teacher's workbook, so all we had to do was teach the lesson for the week, sing some songs, and provide a fun time for the children.

After teaching we'd go to the Pewter Pot, a coffeehouse where I waitressed part time. The fragrance of freshly baked muffins would greet us each time we came in the door. We'd sit there for hours, eating muffins, drinking coffee, and talking. Later we'd leave the cozy atmosphere of the Pewter Pot for dinner at one of our family's homes: meat and potatoes at Tom's house or pasta and Italian food at mine. Most of the time our stomachs were already full of muffins, but we loved being with our families and joining in the lively conversations around the dinner table.

A Significant Meeting

Tom's plans were to go to college at Boston University in the fall. I remember being a bit nervous as September approached, thinking about the sophisticated college girls that Tom would meet while living on campus. Would he forget his little high-school girlfriend back home? But I shouldn't have worried. Tom was so faithful. Even at that young age, he was focused on getting to know me, and he didn't date other girls. Besides, BU wasn't far away, and Tom and I were able to meet frequently.

That same fall a significant meeting took place that altered the course of our entire lives. I had a part-time job after school at the Missile Systems Division of Raytheon. One of the men I worked with was an ex-F-4 navy fighter pilot who had fought in Vietnam.

I knew Tom had always been intrigued with flying, so I asked my coworker if the three of us could meet for lunch. I remember the day so well. It was a crisp fall day, and the leaves on the trees shimmered in brilliant shades of orange and red. Tom picked me up from work, and we met my coworker at a nearby restaurant. We ate quickly, and then Tom and I listened as this ex–navy pilot talked about how much he loved flying high-performance jets. He was so enthusiastic that we hung on every word.

That conversation ignited a spark in Tom—a spark that burned brightly for the rest of his life. He began to research different avenues for becoming a pilot. Eventually he decided that he would enter the navy's Officer Candidate School after he finished college.

I found myself very excited about the prospect of Tom flying. It seemed like such an adventurous lifestyle. Knowing Tom's perseverance, I was sure his dream would become a reality. And if I was going to be a part of that reality, I was ready. I had no fear about Tom flying airplanes. On the contrary, I looked forward to a life spent traveling with Tom.

But I'm getting a little ahead of myself.

True Love

It wasn't until the end of my senior year that I knew for sure, *I really do love this guy!* It was the night of my senior prom. This time I wore a special dress of my own, and Tom wore a beige tux. His ruffled peach shirt matched my peach dress. We looked about the same in this prom picture as we did in the picture two years before. But this time our relationship was very different.

We'd been dating for two years. Even with Tom at Boston

University, we'd been able to see each other frequently and had come to be each other's best friend. I was continually drawn to Tom's character, which was as attractive as his appearance. He was a gentle man, somewhat shy and soft spoken. He never tried to be the center of attention. He wasn't a show-off. I loved his sense of humor, which was never hurtful or off-color. He treated me like a lady. He was respectful, kind, well-mannered.

He may sound too good to be true, but this description is accurate! The entire package of Tom McGuinness swept me off my feet. I went from thinking he was just a gorgeous guy to being amazed that he was so substantial inside.

I came home the night of my senior prom and collapsed on my bed. I stretched my arms out over my head, moaned, and felt warm all over. I was walking on air, bursting with love. Effervescent bubbles danced in my stomach, and I tingled all the way down to my toes with the wonderful knowledge that Tom and I were meant for each other.

I hung my peach prom gown on the back of my closet door and smiled at the thought of a wedding dress hanging there sometime in the future. The euphoria of young love seduced me into a dreamy sleep. A huge part of my future was decided.

The only question I had about Tom and me was a spiritual one. After my Camp Berea experience at thirteen, I'd had very little contact with other Christians who'd had a born-again experience. I did go to church sometimes with my friends Pam and Donna, but I'd really had no consistent teaching or fellowship in all those years. Yes, I enjoyed a solid religious foundation, and I was grateful that my parents raised their children to be responsible, moral people; but my understanding of biblical principles beyond salvation was foggy, and my personal relationship with Jesus hadn't really developed or grown.

I remember wondering, *Is it OK for me to marry Tom if he hasn't had the same spiritual experience I've had?* But my doubts were swept away by my love for him and his assurance that he did believe what I believed about Jesus. And since we both came from religious families and were raised in the same faith tradition, we moved ahead with talk of marriage. I put my born-again thoughts on the back burner.

The Hand of God

I can look back now and see that God was at work in our lives from the very beginning, shaping us to fit the perfect plan he'd always had in mind for Tom and me. I can see that it was God's plan for both of us to grow up in families that lived according to biblical principles. A personal relationship with

Jesus was not talked about in our homes, but our parents worked hard on building godly character in us that would keep our relationship pure until we married and influence every other aspect of our lives.

We went to church, we prayed, we heard the Bible stories and verses that reinforced our parents' teaching. We were taught respect for authority, and we understood that our actions resulted in consequences. If we behaved in godly ways, the results would be positive. If we rebelled, the results would be painful.

Actually, neither of us ever really rebelled. We didn't get into drugs or drinking, and we learned to be comfortable with ourselves early in life. Our identities weren't determined by our peers. In Matthew 7:24–25 Jesus said, "Therefore everyone who hears these words of mine and puts them into practice is like a wise man who built his house on the rock. The rain came down, the streams rose, and the winds blew and beat against that house; yet it did not fall, because it had its foundation on the rock." The biblical values our parents taught us became the rock-solid foundation that protected us in many ways while we were growing up.

In the years that would follow, Tom and I would have our share of troubles; but because of our solid upbringing, we were able to go into our marriage with a basic trust in each other that would carry us through the rough times. We needed to learn to trust God in a personal way, but that would come later. In the meantime, we were blessed by God's guidance and protection— even though we didn't recognize it yet.

JESUS SAID, "LET THE LITTLE CHILDREN COME TO ME,
AND DO NOT HINDER THEM, FOR THE KINGDOM OF
HEAVEN BELONGS TO SUCH AS THESE."

—MATTHEW 19:14

LOOKING AT THE PRINCIPLE

GOD'S PLAN FOR YOU BEGAN TO TAKE SHAPE
BEFORE YOU WERE BORN.

1. Each of us has a spiritual dimension.

Each of us has been given the gift of life by God. We are complex human beings with a physical dimension, an intellectual dimension, *and* a spiritual dimension. That's the way God made us. Our spiritual dimension is a part of who we are. It has been there since before we were born.

As we grow up and our spiritual awareness develops, we begin to ask questions: Why are we here? What's going to happen after this life? Is there a higher being—God—and if so, what does his existence mean to me?

Often our desire to nurture our spiritual understanding is very strong. As we consider these questions and search for answers, we explore different pathways and alternatives. Some of us engage in an intellectual pursuit, trying to understand who God is through reason and logic. Some of us seek to understand him through the practice of organized religion or church activities. And some of us simply search within, trying to find God in our own personal quiet moments.

Ultimately, as we go through life, each of us makes choices that affect the development of our physical, intellectual, and spiritual dimensions. We choose, for example, how much or how little we will exercise, with obvious effects on our physical well-being. Likewise, we make choices about those things we will or will not do to develop ourselves intellectually, again with obvious effects. In a similar way, the choices we make about developing our spiritual dimension have significant, even eternal repercussions. What will we do to nurture and develop our spiritual self? How will we respond to the still small voice speaking within?

2. Family plays a significant role in how our spiritual understanding develops.

What happens in our family of origin clearly has the potential to affect our spiritual understanding either positively or negatively. As we grow up, our family experience either encourages or discourages spiritual growth.

You may have grown up in a family with strong, clearly articulated beliefs and a solid understanding of spiritual things.

Or you may have grown up in a family that substituted moral teaching for spiritual training. You may have been taught to live by the Golden Rule or to obey the Ten Commandments. A relationship with Jesus wasn't really talked about, but very clear and explicit instructions were given regarding right and wrong.

Or you may have grown up in a home where even moral teaching was absent. Your family role models taught you by example that it was OK to do whatever you wanted to do, as long as you could get away with it. They lived by the credo "Do unto others before they do unto you."

Obviously our spiritual development is influenced by the presence or absence of spiritual values and moral standards in our growing-up years. It's also influenced by our family traditions. Did your family attend church every Sunday? Which church? Was Christmas a time for presents and a big meal, or was it a celebration of the birth of Jesus Christ? Was Easter just another Sunday, or did your family acknowledge the sacrifice of God's only Son and the miracle of his resurrection?

Perhaps your family did observe religious rituals. But what was the attitude of your parents in the process? Did they go to church to worship God, or did they feel obligated to be there? Did they say a blessing before meals because they were truly grateful to God for his provision, or because they had grown up saying grace in their own family of origin? Family rituals and religious practices can influence spiritual growth for good or for bad, depending upon the motivation behind them.

3. A biblical foundation for family life can have an enormous, positive effect.

A solid biblical foundation can play a major role in determining how we relate to God and to others. It can help shape our character and influence the type of people we become. It can affect how we view the world and world events, how we deal with life's challenges, and how we make decisions.

Of course, some children are raised in wonderful, godly homes and still turn away from the teaching of their parents. And there are many forms of nonbiblical spirituality that families embrace. But a strong, biblical foundation provides the best environment for seeds of truth to take root and grow in a child's heart.

God's Word gives instructions, guidelines, and directions for living. It gives clear examples of positive character traits and Christlike qualities to emulate. It teaches us how to view the world and our own life circumstances. As parents we may not be able to guarantee what our children will do; but the best option we have, if we want to positively affect their spiritual dimension, is to live in ways that are consistent with Scripture and make biblical principles the foundation of our families.

4. Establishing a biblical foundation for the family takes work.

Establishing a biblical foundation for the family requires leadership. As parents it is our responsibility to lead our families. We do this actively by taking our children to church and Sunday school, participating in regular family Bible studies and prayer times, and encouraging our children in their personal spiritual development. We also do it in more passive ways by being good role models. One of the most vivid memories Tommy and Jennifer have of their father is of waking up early, coming into the kitchen, and seeing him already sitting at the breakfast table studying his Bible. What a wonderful example Tom set for them!

Building a biblical foundation for our families takes commitment. Obviously we have to know for ourselves the principles found in God's Word before we can pass them on to our children. That can only take place through a process of disciplined Bible study and training, followed by practice. Our commitment must be to demonstrate biblical principles in our daily lives; take the time to instruct our children in them; and follow through, follow through, follow through!

He opened the box, took the ring out, and began slipping it on my finger before I could even get "Yes!" out of my mouth.

Chapter Two

TEARS OF JOY, TEARS OF PAIN

Principle 2
GOD KNOWS YOUR FUTURE,
AND HE'S PREPARING YOU FOR IT NOW.

Tom graduated from Boston University in 1981 with a degree in psychology, his dream of becoming a pilot still very much alive. In the fall he headed off to Pensacola, Florida, to attend the navy's Aviation Officer Candidate School. I missed him, of course, but I kept myself busy by taking a heavy course load at the University of Massachusetts.

Marriage was definitely on my mind, but I wanted a career too. I had always admired my mother's devotion to her family, and I definitely wanted a close-knit family life. But competitive sports in high school had put a certain drive in me. And besides,

I wanted to be able to contribute financially to my home.

Tom and I were able to focus on our immediate goals—finishing AOCS for him, graduating from college for me—while keeping our love alive. We wrote letters, talked on the phone often, and spent every minute together when he was home on breaks.

The first Christmas that Tom came home from Officer Candidate School, I thought he might be planning to give me a diamond ring. We'd been dating for over four years, and the timing seemed just right for an engagement. My family knew what I was anticipating, and they joined in my excitement.

My mom cooked for two days straight, preparing her traditional Italian Christmas Eve feast. My sisters and I carried in huge pots for cooking lobster from their storage spaces in the garage. Shrimp, oysters, and clams piled up on the refrigerator shelves. Homemade spaghetti sauce bubbled on the stove, its tangy-scented steam misting into the festive air.

Our home—full of family, food, and old-world tradition—seemed to brim over with the happy anticipation of young love being sealed by a formal engagement. Sometimes I'd catch a little smile creeping over Mom's face while she was cooking. I knew what she was thinking: *My Cheryl is going to get a ring from her Tommy. They are so good together—a match made in heaven!*

The night before Christmas Eve I scribbled "Cheryl

McGuinness" over and over again on a sheet of stationery. My maiden name, Solferino, was so Italian. Now I'd be exchanging one ethnic name for another that was decidedly Irish. I felt a warm, patriotic tingle. *Tom and I are the embodiment of the American spirit*, I thought. *The adult children of two European families, uniting to begin another generation here in the country that welcomes all!* Oh, I was on a lofty, romantic roll!

Christmas Eve finally arrived, and so did lots of aunts, uncles, and cousins. I think every one of them had heard about the special gift that Tom might be giving me.

Finally Tom arrived. When the doorbell rang, I opened the door to see him standing there smiling at me in his blue, tight-fitting disco shirt and blue corduroy jacket. He held a big box in his hand.

Oh, good, I thought. *He's disguised the ring box to surprise me.*

I took the package from him and noticed that it was heavy.

Oh, he really is something! He even put something heavy in the box to throw me off.

Tom was beaming. *Everything is just perfect*, I thought.

We sat down with my family to enjoy the sumptuous meal my mom had prepared. Afterward, we all moved into the family room to open presents. Tom's big box occupied a prominent spot under the Christmas tree.

"Open Tom's gift first," everyone urged.

I sat down on the floor and dragged the box close to me. Smiling, I carefully pulled off the ribbon and paper, making the most of the anticipation. I didn't pay any attention to the advertisement on the box, because I knew the contents were disguised. I pulled the top off.

Cowboy boots!

Cowboy boots?

There was a collective, audible sigh. Tom was the only one who wasn't shocked beyond words.

Expensive, beige-and-brown designer cowboy boots rested in the box in front of me.

I blinked back tears and looked at Tom. He didn't have a clue. He was smiling like a little boy who'd just caught a big fish. I thanked him, hugged him, and moved back from the center of the room.

I went through the rest of the evening like an impersonator. On the inside I was confused and disappointed. On the outside I smiled and helped distribute presents to others, hiding my true feelings. (Only years later did I tell Tom the truth about how I'd felt that night!)

I couldn't stay unhappy for long though. Tom was so good at constantly reassuring me that he loved me and that we would get married one day. Sometimes we would drive around town and fantasize about our future together. We'd pretend that the stuffed animals I kept in a basket in the backseat of my car were our children. We named them "I Love You," "Forget Me Not," and "Sweetheart" (the same names that Jennifer and Tommy and I eventually gave to three of the plants in the memorial spot in our backyard). So much romanticism touched our relationship that I couldn't bring myself to complain about the cowboy boots.

I did cry, though, when I went to bed that Christmas Eve. I was ready to get married, and I wasn't even engaged! This man who was willing to drive around in a car with a basket full of pretend children was so practical that he wouldn't entertain marriage until he could provide for us financially. That meant waiting until he finished AOCS and flight school.

Waiting Awhile Longer

After Tom graduated from AOCS, he transitioned into fixed-wing flight school in Kingsville, Texas. I was still taking a heavy load at college, planning to graduate with a degree in human-resources management by the time Tom finished flight school in the summer of 1983. During that period we only saw each other when Tom came home for brief breaks.

As much as we were attracted to the excitement of Tom's future career, we never needed excitement and high-pitched activity when we were together. Our favorite date was to go to a cheap Italian restaurant, eat dinner, and then talk for hours. So many of our conversations were about our plans for the future. I remember my mom being amazed at how long we would sit and talk.

"Don't you run out of things to say?" she'd ask.

"Oh no, Mom." I'd smile back. "We just love being together. Talking to Tom is easy. I'll never run out of things to say to him."

The following December, when Tom was home on break, he called me two days before Christmas and asked me to come over to his parents' house. His request wasn't unusual; we often hung out there when he was in town.

I arrived at his house and rang the doorbell. It was a typically cold, dark, somewhat dreary New England evening, and I was tired.

"Come on in," Tom called.

I love this guy so much, I thought as I walked in the living room, wowed once again by Tom's sparkling eyes and good looks.

"Cheryl," he said, taking my hands in his, "I have something I want to give you."

He seemed more serious than usual, pensive, even a little excited. He led me down the hallway to his bedroom and closed the door behind us.

"What I want to give you is really special," he said with a trace of a smile peeking out from behind his serious expression.

48

I sat down on the edge of the bed, suddenly grasping what was happening.

Tom dropped down on one knee and pulled out a small box from his pocket. Immediately butterflies took flight in my stomach, and my heart started beating so loud that I was afraid the sound would muffle whatever Tom was about to say.

"Cheryl"—he smiled up at me, tears glistening in his eyes— "will you marry me?"

He opened the box, took the ring out, and began slipping it on my finger before I could even get "Yes!" out of my mouth.

I slid into his arms, crying, mumbling, so excited that this moment had finally arrived. We clung to each other, rocking back and forth on the floor. I could feel his heart beating against mine. It was a moment of pure joy.

We stumbled out into the living room to find his parents waiting for us with big smiles on their faces. I held out my hand to show them my ring, even though they had seen it before I did.

Then Tom and I went over to my house and told my family the good news. I felt as if my arm was permanently outstretched that night, showing off my beautiful, shining diamond. My mom and my sisters hugged me and giggled. They were so happy for me. My dream was finally coming true.

That night as I lay in bed, the tears I shed were tears of joy. Tom and I had loved each other for so long, and now we could look forward to a specific time when we would really be together.

We decided to marry the next summer, after Tom finished flight school and I finished college. That meant another wait—nine more months—but at least this time I had my longed-for ring on my finger.

Tears of Pain

The next nine months were difficult. Tom and I were apart most of that time. My mother didn't like the idea of me, a single woman, flying to Texas to stay with a man—not even when that man was my fiancé. I was swamped with studies anyway, and so was Tom. He came home for visits, but they were always brief.

During that period my family was touched by a terrible sadness: My dad was diagnosed with lung cancer. I was living at school at the time, but I came home as often as I could to help take care of him. Life got even more complicated when my mother had a heart attack while caring for Dad. For a few days, they were both in the hospital at the same time—my dad receiving radiation treatment, my mom recovering from her heart attack. The stress I felt was enormous. How in the world could I finish school, plan a wedding, and help care for my parents, all at the same time?

One day in June, just before I was scheduled to go to Texas to pin Tom's wings on him (the symbol of his successful completion of flight school), my dad became very ill. He had been at home, but now he had to be rushed to the hospital again. I rode in the ambulance with him, holding his hand, worrying that he might not live another month to be present at my wedding.

Once he was stabilized and settled in his hospital bed, I leaned over and said, "You know, Dad, I don't have to make this trip to Texas."

"Oh, I want you to go," he said, patting my hand and trying to smile. His face was ashen and worn. "Tommy is such a good boy. I want you to go pin those wings on him."

His eyes closed for a moment and then opened again with a start.

"I want you to get married," he said. "I want you to do that. And I'm going to be there. If I have to have this oxygen tank attached to me, I'm going to walk you down that aisle. Now, you go to Texas."

"I will, Dad." I smiled through tears.

"I love you," he whispered.

"I love you too."

I kissed his forehead and mouthed a silent good-bye as I backed out of the room. Somehow I knew that Dad wouldn't be at my wedding. But I didn't realize that would be the last time I would see him alive.

The next day I flew to Texas to celebrate Tom's graduation. We were thrilled that he had achieved this great milestone, but our excitement was dampened by the knowledge that my father was dying.

Flying home a few days later, I couldn't stop wondering, *Will my dad still be alive by the time I get to the hospital?* I knew the answer when I saw my sister Patty waiting for me at the Boston terminal. I could tell by the look on her face that she had bad news: Dad had died while I was in the air between Texas and Massachusetts.

When Patty and I drove home, Mom met us at the door, tears streaming down her face. I hugged her for a long time. At that moment I felt more worried about my mother than upset about my dad. I had taken care of Dad, and I'd seen how sick he was. I'd had my chance to say good-bye to him and to tell him I loved him before I left for Texas.

But Mom wasn't ready for this. She had devoted herself totally to her husband and children. She had few friends outside the family, and she had never worked outside the home. She hadn't saved a piece of herself to build a life on now that her children were grown and her husband was gone.

Over the days and weeks that followed, I watched my mom struggle in ways I knew I never wanted to experience. I determined then and there that I'd take my college degree and make a career for myself in case anything ever happened to Tom. I couldn't comprehend living through such a loss; but I knew that if it ever happened, I wanted to survive in a better way than Mom did.

Married at Last

A month later Tom and I got married.

August 6, 1983, was a glorious summer day. I woke up with a sense of disbelief. *How could this day finally be here, after all those years of waiting?* Finally I was going to be Mrs. Thomas McGuinness!

That morning Mom and I went together to get our nails and makeup done. We laughed and talked and enjoyed our last outing together as mother and unmarried daughter.

On the way home, we saw Tom jogging down a street near his parents' house. "Hey, don't you have a wedding to go to?" I called out as we pulled over to the curb.

He leaned into the car, smiling. "I'm working the jitters out," he said. And it must have worked, because he didn't seem nervous just a few hours later at the altar.

We were married in Saint Margaret's Catholic Church in Burlington, Massachusetts, the church we had attended all of our lives. Tom looked debonair in his choker whites, his brass buttons almost as dazzling as his smile. I wore my mother's

white lace wedding dress, with yards and yards of netting flowing out from the front of the skirt. Flowers graced the altar, and
music floated through the air like a canopy of blessings on the
congregation gathered to witness our union.

When Tom kissed me at the end of the ceremony, he lifted
me gently off the ground. At five-foot-three, I was like a feather
in the arms of his strong, six-foot frame. Finally I had been offi-
cially swept off my feet by my Prince Charming.

On Our Own

Tom and I had planned to leave right after our wedding for
Pensacola, Florida, where he would begin his first assignment
as a jet instructor pilot. But daughterly concern filled my heart.
My mom had been my best friend through most of my life. Now
here she was, a new widow, living in a house that echoed with
silence after years of being full of people and life. My youngest
sister was still at home, but she was about to go off to college.
How could I leave Mom under such circumstances?

But my mother encouraged us to move on without regret.
Like a mother hen shooing her chicks with a wave of her
apron, she hushed my concerns with a smile.

"I'll come and visit," she promised.

So Tom and I climbed into our loaded car and headed south.
Our honeymoon was the drive from Massachusetts to Florida,

with stops in Washington, D.C., Virginia Beach, and several other interesting spots.

We arrived in Pensacola refreshed and ready to set up our first household. Real estate prices were favorable for buyers at the time, so we bought a condominium. I loved shopping for curtains, furniture, kitchen gadgets. The work of furnishing and decorating our new home was like a wonderful extended honeymoon.

Sometimes I felt homesick. But just when those feelings would begin to overtake me, a package would arrive from my mom. She knew that Tom and I loved a special salad dressing from one of our favorite restaurants, so she would send us bottles of it. She would fill other packages with pomegranates, persimmons, figs; and at Thanksgiving, different kinds of nuts. Once she even FedExed us a homemade apple pie, one of Tom's favorites.

I took a job as an aerobics instructor, putting off starting my career in human resources since I knew we wouldn't be in Pensacola longer than two years. And what a wonderful two years they were! Tom and I were together, we had no big responsibilities, Tom was doing what he loved, and I was a blissful new bride.

THE LORD YOUR GOD HAS BLESSED YOU IN ALL THE WORK OF YOUR HANDS. HE HAS WATCHED OVER OUR JOURNEY THROUGH THIS VAST DESERT. THESE FORTY YEARS THE LORD YOUR GOD HAS BEEN WITH YOU, AND YOU HAVE NOT LACKED ANYTHING.

—DEUTERONOMY 2:7

LOOKING AT THE PRINCIPLE

GOD KNOWS YOUR FUTURE,

AND HE'S PREPARING YOU FOR IT NOW.

1. From the very beginning of our lives, God knows us intimately.

God created each of us. We enter the world with no conscious knowledge of him, and yet he is the very author of our lives! As Psalm 139:13 says, "For you created my inmost being; you knit me together in my mother's womb." God knows our unique temperaments, our unique strengths, and our unique flaws, because he is the one who made us who we are. And he knows exactly what seeds need to be planted in our lives to bear fruit at just the right time.

"For I know the plans I have for you," God says in Jeremiah 29:11, "plans to prosper you and not to harm you, plans to give you hope and a future." From the beginning of our lives, God is with us, preparing us for the life he alone knows is ahead.

God was always a part of life for Tom and me. I admit that in those early years of our relationship, our faith in him was of a more general nature—not the deep, personal experience we would have later. But God was involved in our lives, using our circumstances—the long years of waiting to get married, the separation, the death of my father—to plant seeds of experience that would bear fruit later.

For example, Tom was deployed on three six-month trips during our marriage, and I don't think we would have handled those periods well if we had not already lived through long separations. The deployments weren't easy, but at least we'd already learned how to love each other from a distance.

Then there was my dad's death—the first deep loss of my life. The shock of his illness brought a sobering reality to our wedding plans. Through that experience I learned that life is not always unspoiled bliss. Painful losses occur right in the middle of wonderful times. That was a lesson God knew I would need to draw on in years to come.

When Tom died, the loss I felt was even deeper, of course. But because I had gone through the experience of Dad's death with my mom, I'd determined early on not to be as dependent on Tom as my mom had been on my dad. That preparation was so helpful when I found myself on my own and the head of my household.

God knew. And all along he was actively involved, preparing us. Preparing me.

2. God's workings in our lives are often beyond our comprehension.

Often we move about our daily lives as if God were not involved with us at all. We are so self-consumed that we give little, if any, thought to how God might be working in our circumstances. I know I've been guilty of this. I didn't realize, for example, that the long separations Tom and I had to endure after he graduated from college were part of God's preparation for our future.

Recognizing and integrating the reality of God's presence into days that unfold in seemingly normal ways is a challenge, even for the best of us. First Corinthians 13:12 says, "Now we see but a poor reflection as in a mirror." God is constantly molding us and conforming us, but our vision is cloudy. Even if we're spiritually astute enough to ask, what is God doing here? we are rarely able to comprehend the answer to that question. We may know in a general way that God is using a particular situation to build our character, but we can't understand why he's going about it the way he is. It's beyond us. That knowledge is his territory.

3. When troubled times come, we can rest in the knowledge that God is aware of our circumstances.

Sometimes when we are in great pain, we feel that God is far away. We cry out to him, but the only answer we hear is silence. We feel abandoned and lost.

But Scripture tells us that God is with us, no matter how we feel. Just because we're unaware of his presence doesn't mean he isn't there. And because he is present, we can be sure that somehow, some way, we will make it through our difficulty. Even if we lose our earthly lives, we will live forever with God in heaven if we have accepted Jesus as our Savior.

Joshua received just such a word from God when he was about to lead the Israelites into the Promised Land. God told Joshua to be strong and courageous, because "as I was with Moses, so I will be with you; I will never leave you nor forsake you" (Joshua 1:5).

Joshua still had to endure troubles. He still had to lead his army against the armies of the north and the armies of the south. But he was able to persevere because God was with him.

Don't turn away from God when you're hurting or discouraged. He hasn't left you, no matter how you feel. He knows your circumstances, and he has a plan to get you through them. Just keep walking with God one step at a time.

4. When God calls, he wants us to answer, what? not, why?

God doesn't always reveal to us why he is doing what he is doing in our lives. But there are many things he does reveal. His Word is full of commandments, principles, and truths that instruct us how to live as followers of Jesus.

We find strength and relief when we focus on doing the things of God we know to do, rather than trying to figure out why difficulties touch our lives. I'm not suggesting that we should stuff our pain or deny it. But so often we get stuck in a fallen position, screaming, why, God, why? when God wants us to trust him enough to get up and take one more step with him . . . then another . . . and another. Instead of, why? we need to ask, what do you want me to do, God? what do you want me to learn in this situation?

I don't believe that my dad's death or the months of separation from Tom happened just so Tom and I could be prepared for events that would happen in the future. But these circumstances did happen as a natural part of life, and God used them later for our benefit.

Nothing is wasted with God. Whatever is happening in your

life right now is precious to him, and he will make sure it serves a purpose. He will bestow blessings on you now and in the future. Yes, some of those blessings will be wrought in the valley of pain. But the pain will lessen, and the blessings will grow as you continue to walk with him.

Tears spilled over onto Tom's cheeks as he pulled me to him and held on. We clung to each other like desperate lovers, finally assured that our long-awaited reunion was actually happening.

Chapter Three

Navigating Life's
Twists and Turns

Principle 3

God is at work in your life,
even when you're too busy to notice.

We'd been in Pensacola about eighteen months when Tom had an opportunity to choose between flying out of a base in Virginia or out of Miramar Naval Air Station in Southern California. We'd always lived on or near the East Coast, so the exotic lure of California drew us in.

I was pregnant with Jennifer when we drove across the country to California. I was excited about becoming a mom, but I was also eager to finally begin my career. I saw no conflict between working and being a mother. Part of the reason, I think, was my growing awareness of the dangers associated with Tom's job. He would be training in F-14s at Miramar, and that would mean learning to land on aircraft carriers in the middle of the ocean. I was excited for him and wasn't consumed with fear, but the image of my mom after Dad died lingered in the back of my mind. What if something happened to Tom, and I had never worked in a job that could support my soon-to-be-born baby and myself?

Tom was supportive of my decision; and once we got to San Diego, I had no trouble finding a job in human resources. When I interviewed, employers could see that I was eager and driven. And my pregnancy didn't raise any red flags because I'd already found a day-care provider based out of a private home. I'd looked at numerous options, checked references, and called licensing boards to clarify regulations before picking what seemed to be the perfect place.

I took three months off when Jennifer was born and loved every minute I had at home with her. At the same time, though, I looked forward to getting back to work. Before long our lives fell into a fast-paced rhythm. Tom was flying, some- times gone for months at a time; I was a full-time working mom. Sometimes my job in employee relations and recruiting called for me to travel to conventions, conferences, and college campuses. The trips were always short, and Tom and I made sure that Jennifer was always with one of us. I must admit, I loved the whirlwind life my job provided.

Married to Mr. Top Gun

Meanwhile, Tom excelled as a pilot and qualified to go to the prestigious navy Flight Weapons School, better known as Top Gun. This happened around the time that Tom Cruise immortalized the elite flight-school pilots in the movie by the same name. Only the cream of the crop have even a shot at being selected for this training. It was exciting, and it was an honor.

Tom's obligation to the navy was complete, and he could have gotten out. But when he talked about taking on the challenge of Top Gun school, his eyes twinkled. I wanted him to experience his dream. Both of us were drawn to the glamour and prestige of such an assignment.

I remember sitting at the kitchen table one night after Jennifer had gone to bed, talking about what Tom becoming a Top Gun pilot would mean to our family. We talked for hours—like the old days at the Pewter Pot. The biggest challenge, for sure, would be the extra six-month deployments on aircraft carriers. How would we handle more long separations? Would Jennifer remember her father when he went away for such extended periods?

We also talked about the danger. We knew that men some-times died young in the fighter-pilot profession. In fact, not long before, a navy friend had flown his plane into the side of a mountain. He had been married with two young children, and now his wife was left to raise her family alone. That could easily have been Tom and me.

Tom was good, though, at reassuring me about his ability. While my own job was a bit of added security for Jennifer and me, I believed Tom when he told me he was a very safe pilot. He wasn't a hot dog who took unnecessary risks. But he did have the qualifications to fly at greater risk levels than most pilots.

I sat at that kitchen table and listened to Tom, my feelings a mixed bag of excitement, anticipation, concern, and fear. I prayed silently, acknowledging that God was ultimately in con-trol. Surely he would protect my husband. *Besides*, I thought, *if something awful does happen, at least Tom would die doing what he loved.*

I could see that Tom was having his own share of butterflies. As he talked he ran his fingers over his short hair. He got up, paced around, sat back down, wrote lists, grabbed my hand.

We both saw a career as an airline pilot as Tom's eventual landing place, and thinking about that future finally clinched the decision. "Being with the airlines will mean straight and level flying," I said to Tom with a smile. "This is your chance to really soar. If you want it, go for it."

So he did.

A Surprise Blessing

Jennifer had been a planned baby. And while raising a family had always been part of the dream Tom and I had shared since high school, Tommy's arrival was more of a surprise blessing. During the latter part of my pregnancy, Tom had to leave on a six-month deployment to the Indian Ocean. Tommy was due several months before Tom would be returning home.

I knew that part of being a navy wife meant accepting the bad with the good. Long separations were the bad part, especially when a baby was due in the middle of that time. To make matters worse, however, my pregnancy was classified as high risk. I was bleeding internally, and according to the doctors, my body was responding as if the baby were a foreign object.

Feeling scared, and with Tom so far away, I took a medical leave of absence from my job and moved back East to live with my mom. She helped me with Jennifer and was a terrific support during those trying months.

When I was eight months pregnant, my girlfriend Donna

took me into Boston for my checkup. The next few hours were miraculous.

"Cheryl," my doctor said with a hint of amusement, "you're in labor."

"What?" I almost yelled. "I don't feel anything—my water hasn't broken—nothing!"

"You're dilated to six centimeters," she said. "You need to go across the street to the hospital right away."

Fifteen minutes after I got into my hospital room, Tommy was born. He weighed six pounds, ten ounces. He was perfectly healthy. In fact, he and I were both just fine, despite the early delivery and the problems I'd had in the pregnancy.

A few minutes after Tommy was born, the phone rang in my room.

"Hi, honey," I heard Tom say, his voice clear as a bell even though he was on an island in the middle of the Indian Ocean.

"Oh, Tom!" I cried.

He had called my mom's house to talk to me, and when she told him I was in labor, he'd called the hospital right away. Our son was only a few minutes old when we were able to share the joy of being parents again, albeit long distance.

The whole process of Tommy's birth was amazing—no problems from the internal bleeding, hardly any pain, an easy delivery.

I thanked God over and over again. My faith was undeveloped, but I felt his presence. I knew he was protecting us.

Another Surprise

Six weeks later Tommy, Jennifer, and I flew back to California. I was going to stay with a girlfriend in San Diego, but when I got off the plane with a toddler, an infant, and a diaper bag, my friend wasn't there.

That was the first sign that things weren't going to go smoothly. My friend, it turns out, wasn't ready for us, and the children and I had to stay in a hotel for a few days. Once we were moved in with my friend, I called my office to let them know I was back in town and ready to return to work. I should have realized that something was wrong when I was put through to my boss. With very little explanation, I was informed that I had been laid off.

Those were frightening, discouraging days. I missed Tom more than ever and tried hard to remember the sense of peace and assurance of God's protection I'd felt at Tommy's birth.

Eventually I started a new job with a major medical-technology firm, Guidant Corporation. I worked at Guidant for thirteen years, moving up through the human-resources department into a managerial position. All the while, a silent battle was going on inside of me. I really did enjoy succeeding at work, but the stress of being a dual-career family was intense. I kept going back to the fact that Tom was in a dangerous business, and my job was a safety net. It would take awhile before all these feelings were fully sifted out and I knew what I had to do.

Daddy's Home

Anticipation bubbled in our little family as the time of Tom's homecoming grew closer. Jennifer was just a toddler, but she loved looking at the calendar we used to mark off the days. We had filled a container with Hershey kisses, one for each day of Tom's deployment, and allowed Jennifer to have one chocolate kiss from Daddy each day. She enjoyed the last chocolate kiss the day before Tom returned. The next day would bring plenty of real kisses, and hugs too.

The day finally arrived. Along with the other wives and children of the dozen pilots who were returning, we drove out to Miramar Naval Air Base and gathered on the airstrip, all decked out in huge smiles, bursting hearts, and our finest attire. Tommy was an oblivious three-month-old, but Jennifer and I were about to jump out of our skins as we watched the skies for the first sight of the planes.

"There he is!" I yelled to Jennifer, pointing to the plane that I knew was Tom's. It was a breathtaking sight—twelve sleek, gorgeous aircraft screaming over us in tight formation. The planes landed and pulled into the assigned places on the tarmac. The canopy of Tom's plane opened and his tall, trim form stood up. Tears filled my eyes as I watched the familiar gait of my high-school-sweetheart-turned-Top-Gun-pilot.

As soon as he reached the point where we could move toward him, we ran toward each other. Jennifer ran ahead of me with outstretched arms. Tom scooped her up, hugging her tight and whispering in her ear.

Then I reached him, holding little Tommy in my arms. Tears spilled over onto Tom's cheeks as he pulled me to him and held on. We clung to each other like desperate lovers, finally assured that our long-awaited reunion was actually happening.

Then Tom leaned back, peered into Tommy's face, and smiled. More tears began to fall. He gently took Tommy from me and stared down into the eyes of his new "little buddy." I picked up Jennifer, and the four of us wrapped ourselves together in a tender embrace on the tarmac. The joy we felt was indescribable.

The next few months of being together again were happy times. Tom and Tommy enjoyed getting acquainted as we adjusted to the new comings and goings of our enlarged family.

It wasn't long after Tom came home that we started to talk about our future. How could we schedule ourselves so the four of us had more time together? Between my job and Tom's flying hours, we didn't have a lot of flexibility. Even though Tom was finally home, the demands of having two careers were still taking their toll.

The decision to leave the navy was a difficult one for Tom. He loved what he did. Flying high-performance jets filled him with tremendous satisfaction. But he also loved his family, and he came to the realization that our lives would be better if he transitioned to a job with the airlines. Many pilots he knew had done just that, and they assured Tom that the schedule was great for a family man. He would fly for a few days and then be home for a few days. He would never be gone for long periods, and he would have several days off in a row to be with his wife and kids.

Tom was a lieutenant commander when he left the navy. He'd been honored and acknowledged in many ways. An excellent pilot with an excellent record, he was able to walk away from the navy with his head held high—and into a new career as a pilot with American Airlines.

Unexpected Pain

One morning in March of 1990, our phone rang. When I answered it, I was surprised to hear the voice of my older sister, Ginny.

"Cheryl," she said in a shaky, tentative voice. My heart started to race. *She has bad news,* I thought.

"Mom is gone," she said. "She died of an aneurysm in her sleep last night."

I couldn't take it in—couldn't believe the words I'd just heard. My mom was only in her midfifties. She was healthy and active. She was going to live a long time. It didn't make sense.

"An aneurysm?" I said, disbelieving.

"Yes, in her heart. It's—"

I interrupted my sister before she could go on.

"But Mom is too young, too healthy. Are you sure?" It was a silly question. But I couldn't accept that my mother was gone—just like that.

I moved through the days and weeks that followed in a numbed state of sadness. I had lost my best friend next to Tom. And it was so unexpected. I couldn't believe that Mom wouldn't be around to see my children grow up, to talk to me on the phone, to send her care packages from home to wherever we were living. Who would teach me how to be a mom?

Tom was a huge comfort, but I realized that the kind of deep comfort I needed could come only from God. In the dark quietness of the night, I prayed to God to help me, heal me.

An Answer to Another Prayer

The experience of losing my mother contributed to our making some needed spiritual changes in our lives. Tom and I had continued to attend Catholic churches after we were married. Both Jennifer and Tommy were christened, and we went on Sundays to whatever Catholic church was nearby. I had told Tom about my experience at Camp Berea as a young teenager, and he was happy for me. However, he didn't understand the concept of a personal relationship with Christ, and he didn't consider it something he needed to pursue. He figured that I needed to have that kind of spiritual experience but he did not. So we just continued to do what we had always done.

Tom approached religious activity as the right thing to do—something to accomplish so you could check it off your list for the week. But I felt more and more eager to go to a church where I could hear the kinds of things I had heard at camp so many years before. I knew there was a dying ember in my heart that was once a flame. I wanted it reignited.

"I'm not getting fed, Tom," I would say to him many Saturday nights. And eventually he agreed that we could break out of our lifelong mold and try some churches in other denominations.

At about this time, we also decided that it was time to buy a new house. So whenever Tom was home on his downtime from American, he would go check out different homes that were for sale. When he found one that he thought might be a possibility, I'd go look at it.

One day Tom asked me to look at a house in an area we were not considering.

"The real-estate agent wants us to look at this one," he said, "and I'm leaving for a trip. Will you go look at it?"

"Why should I go if we aren't interested in that area?" I asked.

"Because the agent is a nice guy who's put in a lot of time with me," Tom answered. "I just want to do it as a favor to him."

The next day Tom took off for his trip, and I went to look at the house. I fell in love with it immediately—and put a down payment on it before Tom ever laid eyes on it. When I called Tom at his hotel and told him what I'd done, he was shocked and a bit amused. He often said that my impulsiveness was one of the things he loved about me!

The location of our new home played a pivotal role in the spiritual quest Tom and I had undertaken. Riverview Evangelical Free Church was only about a mile from our house, so we decided to attend a service one Sunday, not knowing a thing about the church or its denomination. It was our first experience in a Protestant church. I can't say that bells and whistles went off on that first visit, but the thought-provoking teaching of the pastor impressed us, and we liked the experience enough to go back.

Soon Tom's sensitivity took us another step along our spiritual journey. Just as he hadn't wanted to hurt the Realtor's feelings, Tom didn't want to hurt our friend Jim's feelings when he invited us to go to one of Riverview's home-study fellowships.

Reluctantly we drove to the hosts' home that first night, figuring we would go once as a favor to Jim and then back out. We really didn't know what a home-study fellowship was. We had no idea what to expect.

When we arrived, we were greeted warmly and introduced to the dozen or so people who were already there. The group opened in prayer, which intimidated Tom and me terribly. We had never prayed aloud and didn't know what to make of the ease with which these people prayed in front of each other. Then they talked about different scriptures and discussed what they meant. We just watched and listened.

When we got back in the car to drive home, I spoke first.

"What did you think?" I asked Tom.

He hesitated for a moment. "I really don't know what to think, but it fascinated me," he said. "The men in the group seem really, genuinely interested in God."

We went back to the home-fellowship study again and again. In fact, Tom really dove right in. He wanted to be able to participate in the discussions and understand what the group was talking about, so he bought new Bibles for each of us, and we started reading. He read the Bible a lot in his spare time and began studying about Jesus on his own, going beyond the reading the group was doing. He took study material on trips and used his layover times to study. He couldn't get enough of God's Word.

Then one sunny Saturday afternoon, Tom walked into the kitchen and said, "You know, Cheryl, I haven't had any miraculous conversion experience, but something's happened in my heart. I know Jesus is real, and I want to make him Lord of my life. I asked him into my heart today."

I jumped up and hugged him. For years I'd prayed that Tom would accept Christ personally and understand the gospel the way I did! We talked for a little while about how amazing it is to realize that God loves us and wants to be in relationship with us. Then Tom went outside to do something in the yard, and I went into our walk-in closet and dropped to my knees.

"Thank you, God," I whispered through my tears. Then and there I recommitted my own life to the Lord, and the ember that had flickered in my heart for so many years began to grow into a flame. That was the beginning of a new kind of life for Tom and me, with new priorities and a marriage that included God in a more personal way than ever before.

"Be still, and know that I am God; I will be exalted among the nations, I will be exalted in the earth." The Lord Almighty is with us; the God of Jacob is our fortress.

—Psalm 46:10-11

LOOKING AT THE PRINCIPLE

God is at work in your life, even when you're too busy to notice.

1. God patiently waits, watches, and loves as we make choices in life.

God created each of us with a free will and the ability to think, reason, and make choices. Our life journeys are made up of the steps we take as we make innumerable choices and decisions. Some of these choices may seem minor and inconsequential—for example, the decision to take a walk on the beach on a nice summer morning. Others may seem more substantial and monumental, such as the decision of whom to marry. But all of our choices have the potential to significantly impact our lives.

I think back to the seemingly insignificant decision I made to arrange a lunch for Tom and me with my coworker, the former pilot. I can't help but smile at the evidence of God's hand in that meeting! That lunch started a sequence of events that eventually led to Tom's career choice and ultimately resulted in his becoming a Christian. In fact, in hindsight I can see God's hand at work at nearly every turn in our marriage and careers. We didn't see him at the time. We weren't even looking. We made many of our choices without asking for God's direction. But he was there.

Throughout your life journey and mine, God regularly provides us with opportunities to make choices. He continually opens and closes doors. This goes on even when we don't realize it, even when we're too caught up in the moment or distracted by the busyness of our lives to notice. Even when we don't ask, even when we don't see, God is at work. He is watching over us, patiently waiting for us to see him.

2. Sometimes we mistake religious activity for spiritual life.

We sometimes get caught up in the ritual of churchgoing, adopting an "I went to church last Sunday and got my ticket punched" mentality. We mistake religious activity for living a spiritual life.

Even though Tom and I came to understand the meaning of true spirituality, I still find myself on occasion having to make a conscious effort to block out the swirl of activity that typically occurs on a Sunday morning, both in preparing to get to church and during my time in the service. It's frustrating to admit to myself that all my effort, activity, and busyness on Sundays does little, if anything, for my spiritual growth and actually distracts from it.

I've learned that if I want my attendance at church to be spiritually relevant, I have to prepare my mind and heart ahead of time. Many times that preparation is squeezed into the few moments between sitting down in the pew and the start of the service. But whether or not I take just those few moments—to calm my heart and mind and focus on my reason for being there—makes a huge difference. If I don't take this step, I find that my church experience degenerates easily into mere religious activity. If I do take this step, however, I often emerge with my spiritual life refreshed.

3. God often uses circumstances to get our attention.

Tom and I were on a fast-paced roller coaster of our own choosing that provided a consuming diversion to the pursuit of a truly spiritual life. I don't mean this as an excuse; it's just the reality we lived. We had a good life. A happy marriage. Exciting careers. We felt little need for supernatural help.

But eventually the glamour wore thin. Family became a priority, and we knew we needed to raise our children in ways that were consistent with our religious values. Then Mom died, and suddenly finding answers to the deep questions of life and death seemed more important than ever. Before that time Tom and I had been too busy to consider God seriously. Now our busyness wasn't lessened, but our desire for spiritual understanding and nourishment took on a higher priority. Clearly God used the circumstances of our lives to get our attention. He may be using your circumstances to get your attention too.

4. God draws us to himself in many different ways.

At some time in our lives, each of us comes to a point where we stand before God, figuratively speaking. We do it alone. One on one. We make our own choice about whether or not we will respond to him and accept his Son, Jesus. His Word is very clear that no one can accept or reject the gift of salvation for us. We must be the ones to choose. The gift becomes ours, not because we're members of a given church, not because we're associated with a particular group, but solely because we made the choice to accept Christ for ourselves.

God's Spirit moves in us to draw us to himself in different ways. For some the decision to accept Christ mirrors Paul's experience on the road to Damascus—we're literally knocked off our high horse and feel blinded for a time before coming to recognize Christ as our Lord and Savior. For others the decision is the culmination of a slow, steady quest for spiritual understanding—the result of quiet study and internal soul searching.

Each of us is unique, and God works in our individual lives according to his plan and purpose for us. He draws us in the ways that he knows will move us best. Coming to Christ may take place in dramatic fashion. It may be a quiet, slow process. But the result is always the same: He touches the heart, and the heart changes.

If you feel a tug in your heart that may be God drawing you to him, take some time to be alone with him. He may have been wooing you for some time. Ask him to reveal himself to you. Pray for understanding. Open your heart to the God who loves you beyond imagination.

I wondered why I was working so hard and for what. I was only in my midthirties, but I felt as I were having a midlife crisis.

Chapter Four

LOVING GOD'S WAY

Principle 4

GOD CALLS YOU TO BECOME MORE LIKE JESUS BY LOVING OTHERS SACRIFICIALLY.

I thought that when Tom accepted Jesus, our life together would immediately become easier. Any disagreements we had would be quickly resolved. Any issues we faced would be addressed without a struggle. But my desire for instant change didn't coincide with reality. God's flame in my heart was burning again, but there was a lot of competition for my attention.

Mrs. Corporate Executive

My life in those days revolved around my job. I was the one who had to be in an office at a specific time each morning.

Tom's schedule was more flexible. He would be gone for a couple of days, then he'd be off work and at home for four or five days in a row.

Originally I had wanted a career because I thought I needed a safety net. But over time my job began to mean much more. Enticed by the corporate lifestyle, I delved further and further into the world of executive privilege. I traveled from coast to coast to interview potential recruits, visit colleges, and manage the company's booth at job fairs to attract college graduates.

Every morning I transformed myself from a busy mom dressed in robe and slippers, my hair in tangles, to a professional woman draped and styled like a model. My closet racks bulged with expensive, high-power business suits. Dressy shoes occupied several floor racks, and matching purses stood in a line on the shelf above the clothes rack like soldiers in review for their superior officer. My "mommy clothes" were all to one side, arranged with much less precision and ready to be grabbed on a Saturday morning: jeans, T-shirts, sneakers. I didn't wear them much.

On work mornings when Tom was home, I'd help out in the kitchen for as long as I could, then leave him and the kids at the table to finish up with breakfast. If Tom was on a trip, I'd hustle the kids upstairs with me, get them dressed for day care, and set them up with something to play with while I hopped in the shower. Less than an hour later, I'd strap Jennifer and Tommy into car seats, and we'd head off to day care by 7:00 A.M.

I'd drop them off, get back on the road, and my transformation from Mommy to professional woman would be complete. Immediately I'd be in a different world. My mind would jump to my day ahead: What appointments did I have? What problems needed to be solved? What projects needed my attention?

At the office, computer keys clicked and printers hummed. Phones rang constantly like background music. Employee meetings started first thing in the morning and seemed to never end. A stack of professional publications towered precariously on one side of my desk. My mind raced all day long, never bored, always studying the latest material related to my job.

I loved it all. I felt important in the big, wide world of corporate business. I had never dreamed I could be part of so much stimulating activity. The pressure of being in management only fed my feelings of importance. I felt I couldn't leave the office if someone there needed me. How could I say to a troubled employee, "You'll have to wait until tomorrow. I have to go home to my babies"? Being in human resources meant there was always someone who needed help, and most of them had babies at home too.

I tried to ignore the tension I felt by telling myself that my kids were just fine. Jennifer and Tommy were used to my working. It was all they knew. To them it was perfectly normal.

Surely I could have it all: the high-powered job, the wonderful husband, the beautiful home, the perfect kids—the whole worldly dream. But every once in a while, I looked in the mirror and wondered, *Whatever happened to the love-struck girl with the basket of stuffed animal children, leaning on the arm of her knight in shining armor?*

Reality Hits Home

Meanwhile, Tom was busy juggling his job with American Airlines and his role as Mr. Mom. He'd gone from being a Top Gun pilot, with all the attendant glamour and prestige, to being a professional airline pilot who flew the household plane most of the time when his feet were on the ground. To make matters worse for him, we lived in Fallbrook, California, in order to be near my office, which meant he had to endure a horrendous commute from our home to the Los Angeles airport whenever he was flying.

The pressures of being a dual-career family hit me hard when we took a trip to Disney World in Orlando, Florida. I had to attend a convention in one of the Disney hotels and thought it would be great for Tom and the kids to join me. They were so excited! I packed the kids' bathing suits and shorts in bright-colored children's luggage and then watched Tom pack "daddy clothes" with a tinge of envy. My own suitcase was full of business attire: suits, stockings, heels.

Another tinge of envy pricked my heart our first morning in Orlando. Before I went to my first business meeting, Tom and the kids joined me for breakfast. The dining room of the hotel was bustling with families. A few business-types were sprinkled about, sitting alone, but the vast majority of tables were occupied by giggling, chattering moms, dads, and children preparing to set off on exciting family adventures.

I ached inside at the thought of Tom and the kids going off for a day of theme-park fun without me. I wanted to be dressed in shorts and a T-shirt with a camera slung over my shoulder. Instead I was decked out in my power suit with a briefcase by my chair.

I hugged my family and waved to them wistfully as they got on the monorail for the Magic Kingdom. Then, with a heavy heart, I went to my meeting and took my seat in the tightly closed, air-conditioned room with no windows. *Why am I in this box of a room, working, while my family is out playing in the sunshine?* I wondered.

One of the business exercises that day was to answer two questions: "Why do you do what you do?" and "Why is it important?" I could see why my job was important to a certain degree; but the more I thought about it, the more it seemed that it really wasn't *that* important.

The truth was, I had new priorities. God and my family were now first in my life. My lifestyle just didn't reflect that. Was it time for a change?

Growing Pains

As Tom and I grew spiritually, we did begin to change inside. The process was slow, but we became aware of the changes as we got more involved with our home-fellowship Bible study. Tom was a new believer, and I had just recommitted my life to the Lord, so we were the babies of the group.

We were constantly surprised at how much the Bible applied to everyday life. I watched Tom read, take notes, talk to the other men in the group, and then slowly become a more intentional dad and a more loving and gentle husband. His Bible study led him to new conclusions about being a husband and father. Now parenting wasn't just one of many aspects of his life; it was one of the most important aspects, right behind his relationship with the Lord and then with me.

I also watched the other women in the group, and I saw something in them that was both appealing and disturbing. They were good friends to each other and to me—warm, giving, gentle. But I didn't see myself that way. My corporate-executive persona was one tough cookie compared to these loving women, and that bothered me.

I started asking myself questions that had first surfaced at Disney World. I wondered why I was working so hard and for what. I was only in my midthirties, but I felt as if I were having a midlife crisis.

Then the crisis intensified.

I talked to Tom about my job concerns, and we began to discuss the financial challenges that losing one income might present. Then I told Tom about my other growing desire: I wanted to have another baby.

Understand, we had decided sometime after Tommy was born that our family was complete. We adored our children, and we felt we could manage two careers and two children but no more. Now not only was I was thinking about quitting my job, I had changed my mind about having more children. In fact, I was fantasizing about having a new baby all the time. Dirty diapers no longer looked messy, middle-of-the-night feedings seemed idyllic, car seats and strollers looked enticing. My whole body ached to have another child. So what if Tom and I would be parents of a youngster in our forties and fifties?

I'd made a complete turnaround on this subject, but Tom wasn't turning. He thought I had lost my mind. His shock was surpassed only by his determination to convert me to his way of thinking.

The "baby conversation" went on for years. At times I was

really angry with Tom. We didn't yell and scream at each other. But we would talk about having a baby until we were both exhausted.

"I don't want to talk anymore," Tom would say.

"Good. I don't either," I'd reply.

Over time I grew more and more frustrated with our lack of closure, and Tom grew weary of all the repetitive conversations that revealed no new insight. Control, it seems, was a big issue for Tom and me. We hadn't come up against it before, because we had always agreed on so much. Now we were both being challenged to give up control, and it was painful. Neither one of us doubted our mutual love and commitment; but now our love and commitment were being tested to the point of personal surrender. Clearly, one of us was going to have to give up his or her own agenda.

Bringing God In

Finally we decided to go for counseling with our pastor, Dr. Larry Grine. He'd had a big influence on Tom when Tom first accepted Christ, and he knew us well.

In our first counseling session, we told Larry about our years-long struggle. He listened intently, nodding and softly smiling. Then, over the course of several visits, he talked to us about loving each other enough to give up our own desires. He talked about real love—Christlike love, sacrificial love.

With Tom he talked about being willing to have another child out of love for me. Larry explained to Tom that he didn't want any more children either (he and his wife, Annie, have four boys), but if Annie came to him and said that she wanted another baby, he would be willing to become a father again out of love for her. Of course, decisions aren't that simple, he explained, but love was the bottom line.

Then Larry talked to me about the change of heart I needed to make. It would take time, he said, but I needed to be willing to make a 180-degree turn. He understood that my heart's desire for a baby was huge, but I had to be willing to let God change my heart. I needed to be willing to accept whatever God wanted for me, knowing that he loved me and wanted the best for me.

After those counseling sessions, Tom and I talked for hours, whenever we could find the time—after Jennifer and Tommy were in bed, on dinner dates, during free time on the weekends. The level of our communication deepened as we put into practice the techniques we learned from Larry. We learned to be good listeners and to go to the Scriptures together. And ever so slowly, we learned the meaning of sacrificial love. We learned how to let go of things we once thought we just had to have. We learned to replace our desires with a desire to have God's will be done.

The often-quoted passage from 1 Corinthians 13 convicted me about my controlling attitude. It says: "Love is patient, love is kind. It does not envy, it does not boast, it is not proud. It is not rude, it is not self-seeking, it is not easily angered, it keeps no record of wrongs. Love does not delight in evil but rejoices with the truth. It always protects, always trusts, always hopes, always perseveres. Love never fails" (1 Corinthians 13:4–8). I could read those words in a few brief moments; but putting them into practice, especially in this area of my life, took years.

Eventually after much discussion, hand-wringing, counseling, prayer, and finally relinquishment, Tom and I came to a place of closure. We decided to simply trust God. We wouldn't focus on getting pregnant. If God blessed us with a baby, that would be great; if he didn't, that would be fine too.

Amazingly, my consuming desire to have another baby subsided. Tom's openness to the possibility of a larger family grew. But we stopped talking about it and stopped trying to manipulate the outcome. We felt a sense of relief and wonder at the way God had entered our decision-making process and changed our hearts. Our personal desires were still there, but the intensity was gone. Our love for each other and our desire to have a godly relationship became the priorities of our marriage.

One More Transition Step

The baby decision was taken care of, but my work scenario was still in flux. I wanted to quit my job, but we'd gotten used to living on two incomes. Tom and I talked about trying to downsize our lifestyle and progress toward becoming a one-income family. If I stopped working, we'd need to make some pretty drastic changes.

Then an intermediate step presented itself.

Part of my job in human resources was to create programs to help people balance their work lives and their family lives. Many corporations at that time were beginning to use telecommuting to achieve this balance for some of their employees, enabling those employees to do all or part of their jobs from their homes. The employees would communicate with their offices by means of phone, fax, e-mail—whatever electronic means were available. I decided to design a program to see how that option would work for my own company.

I asked my boss if I could try telecommuting myself, and he agreed. Jennifer and Tommy were in school by this time, so my days were uninterrupted. I was very productive and loved my newfound flexibility. I could be with the kids and Tom before they all left in the morning, and I didn't have to worry about getting myself dressed by a certain time. I often wore my white, fluffy bathrobe and my bunny slippers well into the day. I could throw in a load of laundry in between business calls.

Telecommuting worked really well most of the time. Then one day when Tom was home, the stress of my job grew to be too much for him. I was on an important phone call, and Tom walked into my home office. He stood there, waiting. I knew the call was going to take some time, so I excused myself on the phone, put my hand over the mouthpiece, and looked questioningly at Tom.

"Can you go to lunch with me?" he asked in a nonchalant way.

"Are you kidding?" I responded in a shrill whisper. "I'm on a big call. I can't just drop it and go!"

Tom turned and left my office without another word.

That night he said, "Cheryl, we've talked about this long enough. You should quit your job."

That was all I'd been waiting for: I wanted Tom to be in agreement with me about leaving my job. I was willing to work until he got to that point, so we were never at a serious impasse. This was much different than the baby question. But now that Tom wanted me to quit, I felt delight and relief. I was definitely ready.

The next day was February 14. My Valentine's Day present

to our whole family was my resignation. I went into my boss's office, gave one month's notice, and began to transition out of my job for good.

My happiness was dampened a bit that day by doubts that crept into my thinking. I had never been totally financially dependent upon Tom. I felt OK about the drop in income that was coming, but I was apprehensive about what life would be like for me personally. Would I have to ask Tom for allowance money? I knew he wouldn't treat me like a child, but what exactly could I expect?

That night Tom and I went to a sweetheart banquet at our church to celebrate Valentine's Day. After the meal Pastor Larry stood up at the front of the room with his wife, Annie. He asked everyone to stand and told the men to put their arms around their sweethearts. When Tom wrapped his arms around me, tears started spilling down my face. He was so loving and strong and committed to me and the children. *I don't have to worry*, I thought. *This change is going to be good for all of us.*

Then Larry led the group in vows of recommitment to our marriages. Tom looked down at me and said his vows, pledging before God to be the kind of husband that God wanted him to be. I couldn't even speak when it was my turn. I just looked up at Tom and cried. He knew what was in my heart and held me close to him.

After this part of the renewal ceremony, Tom handed me an envelope.

Inside were tickets for a hot-air balloon ride for Tom, me, Jennifer, and Tommy.

"It will be like a second honeymoon," Tom said, "with two additional guests."

The next day the four of us piled into the balloon basket and sailed out over the Pacific Ocean off the Southern California coast. We hugged each other and thanked God for the beautiful place he had given us to live. We felt so happy and settled.

A Surprise Decision

Now that I was quitting, we realized we had an opportunity to make life a little easier on Tom by moving closer to the airport. Tom heard that American Airlines had openings for pilots based out of Boston; but our focus at that point was on moving closer to Los Angeles, not cross-country.

Over the years Tom and I had thought about moving back to the Northeast, but we'd never seriously pursued the idea. A seed had been planted, though, the previous year when Tom met Chris Hoag, a Christian pilot who lived in Portsmouth, New Hampshire, about an hour's drive north of the Boston airport. They'd found themselves together on a six-hour flight; Chris was piloting and Tom was "deadheading" (an airline term meaning he was not working the flight but sitting in the extra seat in the cockpit). The two new friends spent most of the time talking about what it was like to live in Portsmouth. As Chris spoke Tom took copious notes.

Tom came home that night full of information about the great place to live he'd just heard about—near our hometown, great Christian school, good real-estate values, on and on. We didn't dwell on it, though, figuring that a move wasn't on our radar screen. But thoughts about Portsmouth resurfaced in June of 2000, a few months after I quit my job.

Jennifer and I flew back to Massachusetts to visit one of my sisters. "Why not take an afternoon and drive to Portsmouth to check it out?" Tom had suggested. So we did.

We met a Realtor who showed us around many different neighborhoods in the Portsmouth area. The houses looked so old in comparison to the new California-style homes we were used to. The last neighborhood we visited was different, however. The homes were newer but still built in the traditional style: lots of brick, shutters, two stories, long driveways, big trees. They were beautiful and charming at the same time.

Just as we were leaving the neighborhood, Jennifer cried out, "Oh, Mom, look at that one!" She pointed to a house that was picture-postcard pretty, two-story brick with black shutters. Big trees framed the house, and flowers lined the winding driveway. It wasn't for sale, though, so we just admired it from the street and drove on.

Through the rest of June and the month of July, Tom and I prayed and prayed about where we should live. Our home had sold on June 1, and we'd been in a rental since then. The next school term was closing in, so for the kids' sakes, we knew we needed to decide something. Would we move closer to LAX or back to New Hampshire?

Finally Tom knew what he wanted to do: go back East. I felt uncertain, but I trusted his judgment.

Over the course of a few weeks, Tom got the transfer to Boston, we registered Jennifer and Tommy at Portsmouth Christian High School, and our family moved into a hotel suite in Portsmouth, New Hampshire, where we lived for nine weeks. Then—who would have guessed it?—the house that Jennifer and I had seen and admired back in June went on the market. So we bought the pretty brick house with black shutters, overhanging trees, and flowers lining the long, winding driveway.

A new, exciting chapter in our lives had begun.

I HAVE BEEN CRUCIFIED WITH CHRIST AND I NO
LONGER LIVE, BUT CHRIST LIVES IN ME. THE LIFE I LIVE
IN THE BODY, I LIVE BY FAITH IN THE SON OF GOD,
WHO LOVED ME AND GAVE HIMSELF FOR ME.

—GALATIANS 2:20

LOOKING AT THE PRINCIPLE

GOD CALLS YOU TO BECOME MORE LIKE JESUS BY
LOVING OTHERS SACRIFICIALLY.

1. Godly decision making as a couple takes work.

Sometimes, as Christian couples, our desire to make godly decisions is hampered by our expectations of the other person. We assume that since both partners are Christians, we will automatically be like-minded about everything.

But even though two people believe the same thing about Jesus, they still have their own unique thoughts, understandings, desires, and expectations about life. In all likelihood their biblical knowledge and spiritual maturity are at different levels. Their experience with God and rate of spiritual growth are probably different. These differences can be a real source of strength, as couples recognize their respective gifts and learn to complement one another. They can also be a real stumbling block.

That's why the first step in involving God in a couple's decision making is commitment to the process. Both partners have to accept the fact that changing the way they make decisions will take work and practice.

For me the process always involves a number of steps. First, after making a commitment to the process of change, I need to learn what God's Word says about the specific issue, about decision making in general, and about sacrificial love. I need to ask, Is there clear instruction in the Bible about the particular question or problem? Have I studied God's Word enough to fully understand sacrificial love?

When Tom and I were trying to decide about having another baby, the defining moment for me came when I read about God giving his Son as a sacrifice for us. From my perspective as a mother, such an act seemed unimaginable. But as I came to appreciate what it would mean to offer your child as a sacrifice for someone else, I realized how much God must truly love me. That understanding brought me to the point of being willing and able to sacrifice my own desire for another baby so that Tom might have his desire met.

Second, once I learn what God's Word says, I need to step out in faith to make a decision, trusting God for the result. I also need to trust him to give me peace and joy if that outcome is not what I originally wanted.

After I learned what the Bible had to say about sacrificial love, making the decision to let go of my own desire for a baby brought me not only tremendous feelings of peace, but also true joy and an even deeper experience of love for Tom. I didn't get the outcome I'd wanted so badly, but God was faithful to give me so much more.

2. God uses people and circumstances to help us grow.

God raises up and equips his people to do his work. Many of us have been fortunate enough to have people in our lives who have taught us biblical truths. When Tom and I were new Christians, Pastor Larry at Riverview Church was probably our most influential teacher. His input was critical in helping Tom and me learn how to involve God in our decision making as a couple. Pastor Larry's teaching equipped us so that we, in turn, could begin to equip Tommy and Jennifer.

Our pastor's teaching also prepared so many other members of the body of Christ at Riverview. This church family, properly equipped and raised up, provided untold and immeasurable comfort, support, and love to me and my children after 9/11. Even from the other side of the country, their labors of love, their individual efforts and kindnesses, gave witness to the biblical principle of the body ministering to its members.

3. Godly decision making requires sacrificial love.

Tom and I had both accepted Christ as Lord and Savior of our lives. We were both committed to having Christ as the center of our relationship. But when it came to the decision of whether or not to have a third child, we were stuck. We both had well-reasoned, practical arguments for what we believed. We both felt that God agreed with our respective arguments. We both wanted what we wanted. We were at an impasse.

Only when Tom and I invited God into the decision-making process and determined to seek his will above our own were we finally able to move forward. Getting to that point required each of us to be patient, loving, and accepting. It required us to be humble and to put aside our personal wants and desires. We needed to be willing to listen to each other, seek what was best for the other person, and accept the outcome, whatever it might be. Only by understanding and seeking to emulate Christ's example of sacrificial love were we able to break through.

4. The results of learning to love sacrificially are joy and peace.

When we are able to get past our personal wants and desires, godly decision making becomes so much easier. And in this, as in so many areas of life, success breeds success. I have found that as I do trust God for the result in a particular situation, it becomes easier to trust him in subsequent circumstances.

I have also found that godly peace and joy are the result of this kind of godly decision making. My experience with the "baby decision" showed me that it is possible to experience true joy, even when the result is not what we think we want.

I didn't just reach a point of begrudging acceptance. Over time my heart actually changed, and I found peace. My own desire to have a baby diminished as I focused more on loving Tom. And as Tom also let go of his own desires, we grew closer, much closer. Our selfish desires were given to the Lord, and he blessed us with a greater love for each other. We learned the meaning of sacrificial love and experienced the amazing joy of loving each other in a deeper way than we ever thought possible.

That experience of learning to trust God and be at peace with whatever outcome he allows had great significance for me after Tom died. Many people have asked me how I have come to terms with the loss of Tom. I tell them honestly that, yes, I miss him. I miss him so much.

But I also tell them that God has given me the ability to accept my life here without Tom. He has helped me accept the fact that Tom is in a better place. He has given me peace about that—enough peace, in fact, that I can honestly say, "No, I wouldn't want Tom to come back."

I know that my time here on earth is relatively short, and one day Tom and I will be reunited. He just got a head start on eternity! God has enabled me to sacrifice my desire to have Tom with me now in order to have what is best for him. And I have immeasurable joy and peace knowing that my beloved husband is with his Savior, Jesus.

We did not walk through the valley of the shadow of death alone. God was with us through all the wonderful people he brought into our lives. He still is.

Chapter Five

GOD'S HANDS AND FEET

Principle 5

GOD WANTS YOU TO EXPERIENCE HIS LOVE
THROUGH THE LOVING CARE OF HIS PEOPLE.

On the evening of September 10, 2001, we celebrated Tom's forty-second birthday, just the four of us—me, Tom, Jennifer, and Tommy. I spent the whole day preparing our special meal, which included a nonfat cheesecake. After dinner we stuck a candle in the cake and sang "Happy Birthday." Jennifer gave Tom a "love certificate" promising that the two of them would go out sometime to a favorite Italian restaurant. Tommy's gift was the promise of working in the backyard with Tom for a day, cleaning up the woods and chopping down a couple of trees.

We were so grateful for the goodness of God that was so evident in our lives.

My daily routine delighted me. I relished the time I had now to spend with Jennifer and Tommy, to fuss around the house, to make Tom's homecomings from trips special, to read and study and reflect, and to simply be Tom's wife. The pace of life was pleasant and full; busy, but not frantic.

On many mornings I'd take the kids to school, come home, and sit out on the back deck with a cup of coffee and my Bible, just as I did on the morning of September 11. Our backyard is full of tall trees, shielding us from the outside world like protective sentinels; so while the house is close to town and surrounded by other houses, the trees provide us with a private outdoor haven. It's the perfect arrangement: People are close enough to form community, and yet we can retreat to a peaceful place just outside our back door.

Friends Near and Far

We were the new kids in town, both in church and in the neighborhood. When we first arrived, I had no idea how long it would take for us to feel at home, to become involved, to make new friends—the kind of great friends we'd had in Fallbrook. I'd often heard about the coolness of people from the Northeast. But in our experience, that characterization never rang true. Maybe that's because Tom and I grew up in the area. We found the people in Portsmouth to be warm and inviting.

A few months after our move, a couple on our block asked us to join a couple's Bible study with several other husbands and wives from our new church. We were amazed to have so many Christian people around us so quickly. Tom and I were asked to lead the study soon after we joined, but we declined. Because of his flight schedule, Tom couldn't guarantee that he would always be home when the group met. We ended up agreeing to co-lead the study with the original leaders.

In addition to the couples study, I got involved in a neighborhood women's Bible study and a city-wide community Bible study that met in our church building. After having spent so many years working, I was eager to be with other women during the day who were studying the Bible. I just couldn't get enough of those times.

Tom and I also had opportunities to meet and become friends with many of the parents from Portsmouth Christian High School. Jennifer and Tommy were involved in a number of extracurricular activities, and we got to know the parents of the other kids who were involved in the same things. Our circle of friends had grown wider than we ever could have imagined in such a short period of time.

Little did we know that these new friends were soon to

become the hands and feet of Jesus in my life.

The events of 9/11 happened just a little over a year after we moved to New Hampshire. The outpouring of help and support that the children and I received from our friends following the terrorist attack was beyond my ability to comprehend.

In the early days, I moved around in a fog, unaware of who was doing what; but later I was able to look back and see just how many people had pitched in and helped out. There were women cleaning my house, doing the laundry, making meals, helping me write thank-you notes. Not one need went unaddressed.

Then expressions of sympathy began to come in from all across the country. Flowers, baskets of fruit, teddy bears, and other gifts arrived by the dozens. We heard from close friends, faraway friends, and people we'd never even met before.

One day a woman came to the house with a check for me. She explained that she had been recuperating from hand surgery when she'd seen the events of 9/11 on television. In the days that followed the tragedy, this dear woman stitched together little American flags, which she then sold outside her local Wal-Mart. She made four hundred dollars, and now she wanted to give it all to me.

I held that check in my hand and cried. What an amazing offer of love from a stranger—delivered in person no less!

Another lady wrote and told me a story about Tom that made me smile inside and out. She had flown on American Airlines Flight 11 with her grandson one month before September 11. They were going to Disneyland, and her grandson was very excited about the trip and about flying in a big jet.

At some point Tom came out of the cockpit and asked the little boy if he wanted a pair of wings (the little ones the airlines sometimes give to children on flights).

"I already have some," the youngster replied.

"Then can I pin these wings on your teddy bear?" Tom asked, looking down at the stuffed animal nestled in the little boy's lap. The boy smiled and nodded yes, and Tom pinned the wings on the bear. The lady went on to say that Tom spoke to other children on the flight, too, and that all of them loved their visit from the pilot. What a gift it was for this woman to write to me and let me know how Tom had touched many children's lives only the month before!

Another meaningful gift we received was a beautiful handmade quilt that five or six special women put together. Our family scripture was on it: "But if serving the LORD seems undesirable to you, then choose for yourselves this day whom you will serve. . . . But as for me and my household, we will serve the LORD" (Joshua 24:15). Tom had discovered this passage one day during his study time, shortly after we'd moved to

New Hampshire, and he had announced to the rest of us that this would be our family Bible verse. We'd even held a family ceremony and dedicated our home to the Lord. The quilt is a wonderful, visible reminder of the God-centered home Tom helped to build.

Going the Extra Mile

Of all the gifts we received, it's hard to qualify any one as better than the others. To me they all represent the goodness of God reflected in the hearts of his people. I am grateful for every person who sent a note or a gift or expressed sympathy in any way. I wish I could respond personally to each and every person who reached out to us.

A few people we'd never known before became good friends in the aftermath of 9/11. For example, we met John and Lynn after being interviewed on the morning news show *Good Morning America.* During the interview Tommy had talked about the quiet moments his father had liked to spend with him at the end of the day, just talking and telling him he loved him. Sometime after that broadcast, Lynn, whom I'd never met before, called the house and began to tell me about her husband, John, watching the interview. She told me that John had been very moved by Tommy's words and demeanor. He felt a deep sorrow for this young man losing his father.

We were about to end the conversation when Lynn asked if she and John could do something special for us for Christmas.

"John is a talented woodworker and could make something really special," she said.

"Thank you, but that's not necessary," I responded.

Lynn insisted. She was so sweet and kind and genuine. So I told her that Tommy had some models of F-14s that he would love to display. He had been wanting some kind of special shelf, and we hadn't gotten around to looking for one. Lynn enthusiastically promised that John would make a shelf for Tommy.

That one shelf grew into an entire project. Not only did John make a number of individual shelves for the F-14 models; he also made two long shelves to display Tommy's sports trophies.

Lynn and John went to church with us one Sunday morning and then came over to the house to put the shelves up. John and Tommy worked together while Lynn and I talked. A friendship began that I continue to value today. Lynn is a wise woman who knows God and shows his love to those around her. I didn't even know her before the September tragedy, but now I love her dearly as a friend in the Lord. She showers me with what she calls "smotherly" love.

Jackie is another woman who has shown God's goodness to my family. Jennifer and Tommy call her Grandma Jackie, which she loves to hear. She's involved with the senior-high youth group at church. It's so much fun to see this older woman relate so well to teenagers! And it's good for them to know and respect an elder in a day when so many younger people don't seem to appreciate the wisdom and gifts of older people.

Jackie and I had a special breakfast one morning when I was feeling particularly low. Tom had been gone for over a year, and I felt stuck. I wanted to talk to someone who had been walking with the Lord a long time and could give me the perspective of many years of wisdom. That's when Jackie called and asked me to go to breakfast with her. We talked for a long time, and her graciousness touched my soul.

Bonnie, a dear friend from California, is another older woman whose friendship I treasure. Tom and I used to call her our California mom. Jennifer and Tommy call her Grandma Bonnie. She flew to New Hampshire for Tom's memorial service and again for the first anniversary of Tom's death. Her very presence was and always is a comfort to me. Having lost my own mother, the wisdom and comfort I receive from older, godly women fill a deep need.

Help When the Media Descended

When I first agreed to do radio and television interviews, I called everybody I knew and asked them to pray for me. Pastor

Larry in California promised that he would fast and pray. I was so nervous! During one of those first interviews, I had two of my girlfriends, Vicky and Rebecca, come to the house. I was worried about how the house looked, what I was wearing, and more importantly, what I would say. Then the television crew rushed in and started to move furniture around. My immediate thought was, *Oh no, there's dust under the sofa.* Soon yards of cables crisscrossed the family-room floor. High-powered lights pointed to the spot where I'd be sitting. I was a wreck!

Thankfully, Vicky and Rebecca helped calm me down. They sat with me in my bedroom, and we prayed together. They even said funny things to make me laugh. When I finally began the interview, I was calm. The words just came. I had peace knowing that I was doing what God wanted me to do. To this day, when I look at the tape of that interview, I am amazed. I don't look broken. On the contrary, I look whole, almost beaming. Clearly God was at work, restoring me and preparing me to be used in a new way.

It took several months before I felt confident enough to do an interview without a friend being with me. In those early days, my friends helped carry me through the interviews— and all the other new experiences that were fast becoming part of my life. God's goodness shined through them, and I am grateful.

In fact, I have much to be grateful for. From the moment Tom was taken from our family until this very minute, many wonderful people have helped to lighten the burden for Tommy, Jennifer, and me. We did not walk in the valley of the shadow of death alone. God was with us through his Holy Spirit, and he was with us through all the wonderful people he brought into our lives. He still is. Even now, remembering those people encourages me.

I shudder to think how I might have responded to September 11 if God had not been such an intricate part of my family's life. On our last night together, Tom and I had spent time reflecting on God's goodness. These days I often spend time doing the same thing. I love to sit quietly and think about the amazing love of Christ. Whenever fear creeps in and tries to defeat me, I stop and think of all the goodness that has flooded my life these past few years. And then I can go on.

Top: Cheryl's dad and his girls. *Left to right:* Ginny, Linda, Patty, and Cheryl (front), 1968.

Bottom: Tom, first grade, 1965.

Cheryl and Tom at senior prom, 1979.

Tom and Cheryl while in high school, 1979.

Cheryl and Tom while dating, 1979.

Cheryl pins wings on Tom at his flight-school graduation, 1983.
(During her flight home, her father dies.)

Tom and Cheryl's wedding, August 6, 1983.

Top: Tom McGuinness, 1985.

Left: Tom proudly holds his six-month-old daughter, Jennifer, December 1985.

Top: Cheryl and Tom with Tommy (age 2)
and Jennifer (age 4), 1989.

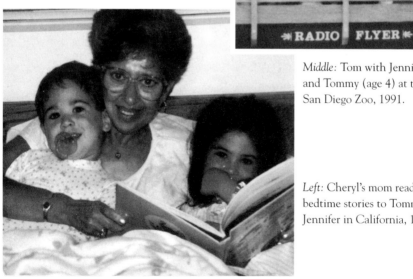

Middle: Tom with Jennifer (age 6)
and Tommy (age 4) at the
San Diego Zoo, 1991.

Left: Cheryl's mom reading
bedtime stories to Tommy and
Jennifer in California, 1989.

Top: Tom and Cheryl, 1992.

Bottom: Tom and children outside their home in Vista, California, 1992.

Top: Tom McGuinness,
Top Gun fighter pilot, Miramar
Naval Air Station, 1990.

Right: Tom McGuinness,
Navy fighter pilot, Miramar,
San Diego, California, 1993.

Top: Tom comes home to Jennifer (age 11) and Tommy (age 9), 1996.

Bottom: Tom's cockpit birthday party, August 2001.

Top: Tom, Cheryl, Jennifer, and Tommy at a family apple-picking, September 2000.

Bottom: Cheryl and Tom with fellow members of their small-group studies in Fallbrook, California, 2000.

Top: Tom and Cheryl at Pilgrim Pines Family Camp, July 2001.

Middle: Tommy and Jennifer at Pilgrim Pines Family Camp, July 2000.

Left: Tommy, Cheryl, Jennifer, and Tom, June 2001.

From Cheryl's scrapbook
(For photo credit, see page iv)

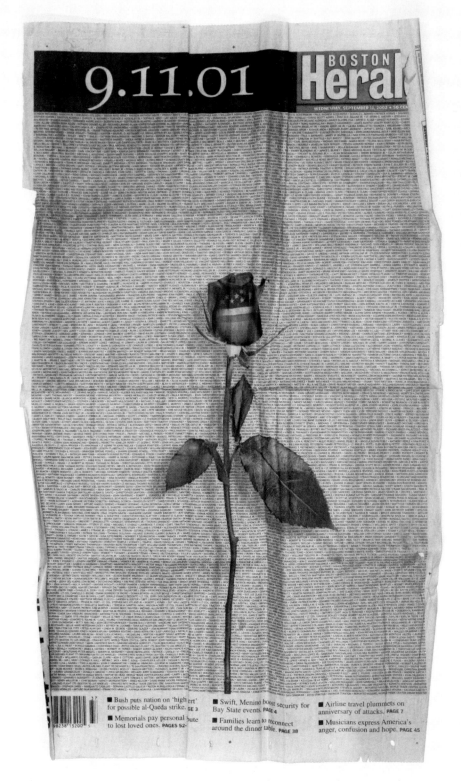

Cheryl's "Love Letter from God," found at Rye Beach, New Hampshire, September 2002.

Right: Jennifer, Tommy, Cheryl, and Ally, Christmas 2001.

Bottom: Jennifer, President Bush, Cheryl, and Tommy at the University of New Hampshire, 2002.

Top: Memorial tree planting at Portsmouth, New Hampshire, Post Office, September 11, 2002.

Bottom: Edie and Tom McGuinness Sr. (Tom's parents) with their five grandchildren.

Top: Jennifer, Tommy, and Cheryl McGuinness, 2004.

Bottom: Cheryl giving President Bush a copy of *Beauty Beyond the Ashes*, 2004.

BUT BE SURE TO FEAR THE LORD AND SERVE HIM
FAITHFULLY WITH ALL YOUR HEART; CONSIDER WHAT
GREAT THINGS HE HAS DONE FOR YOU.

—1 SAMUEL 12:24

LOOKING AT THE PRINCIPLE

GOD WANTS YOU TO EXPERIENCE HIS LOVE
THROUGH THE LOVING CARE OF HIS PEOPLE.

1. God can use anyone.

The work of God is usually accomplished by people.
Individuals. Members of God's church called by name to meet
someone else's need.

My experience after 9/11 was that, time and time again,
individuals stepped in to minister and care for me and my children. And that work was not done only by people from the
local body, our church. God used the larger, universal body of
believers to minister to us too. He used individuals who lived
next door, across the country, and around the world. He used
people we knew before the tragedy and people we'd never met
before that day.

So many people reached out to us that it is impossible to
name them all. But their care was overwhelming evidence to us

of God's love. We watched as God used people from all walks of life—people who were experiencing all kinds of circumstances themselves—to meet our needs. Through this experience we learned that any of us can be chosen by God to help others; any of us can be called upon to be the hands and feet of Jesus. That's exciting!

2. We need to accept the help of others.

It's not always easy to accept help. Sometimes we're hampered by pride or an independent streak that says, "I can take care of myself." Sometimes we're afraid of change; other times we're reluctant to shed our victim status. Learning how to accept help when it's offered is a crucial step on the pathway toward healing and wholeness.

The months since 9/11 have been an ongoing process of healing and recovery for me. Sometimes I wonder if it will ever end. Will I ever be fully healed? But I have made progress—and learning to accept the help of others has played an essential role. Yes, at times it has been humbling. At times my independent, self-sufficient streak has struggled against the cold, hard reality of my need. But through the process of learning to accept help, I've experienced healing that I never would have achieved any other way.

3. We need to be sensitive to the needs of others.

We need to keep our eyes and our minds open to recognize the needs that exist all around us. Then we need to listen for God's quiet call and be willing to respond when he prompts us to reach out.

Too often we walk right past needs without noticing them. I know I'm guilty of this kind of selective blindness. I like to believe I miss these things because I'm overly busy, not because I'm self-absorbed. But I know that when I do take the time to stop, look, and listen, God is quick to point out the needs of others and open up opportunities for me to minister in his name.

One of the most meaningful educational experiences I had along these lines took place when I walked into our local Salvation Army office several weeks after Tom died. I had been struggling to understand my healthcare benefits, and a friend had suggested that I call the Salvation Army office for help.

The people there were wonderful. With their knowledgeable assistance, I was able to sort through all the paperwork and get my questions answered. For years I had given donations to the Salvation Army—clothes, money, "stuff." But this time I saw the other side of their ministry. I saw people in need. I was one of them. It was an experience I will never forget.

God used my visit to the Salvation Army to help me understand: No one chooses to be in the position of needing help. But when you are in that place, you are thankful for those who have listened to God's voice and responded to his call.

4. Ministry to others can be accomplished in the simplest ways.

Sometimes we get stuck believing that ministering to others requires some kind of grand program. We think if our service isn't part of a big ministry or accomplished through some bold and miraculous event, it doesn't count.

My experience after 9/11 taught me just the opposite. So many people stepped in and did so many different, little things to lighten our load. I cannot begin to count the number of times someone showed up unexpectedly with a meal. Others simply stopped by for a cup of coffee and to chat. Still others just seemed to arrive at exactly the right time, right when we needed someone to be there. Immediately after September 11, many of my sisters in Christ from Bethany Church stepped in to help me with the daily household duties that were beyond my ability to get done at the time. They did my laundry, cleaned my house, drove my children to school—all the ordinary chores that are so extraordinary when someone else does them for you!

Over and over again, God has shown me that he uses his people, his church, to extend his love to us and minister to each of us at our point of need. Our part is to be sensitive to his leading, ready to respond, and willing to do whatever it takes—even if it's the simplest thing—to bless someone else in his name.

"Tom was undoubtedly one of the finest officers I have ever served with in my twenty-four-year navy career."

Chapter Six

BUILDING FOR TOMORROW

Principle 6

GOD DESIGNED YOUR LIFE
TO HAVE AN IMPACT ON ETERNITY.

I'm sure Tom didn't anticipate leaving this life at the age of forty-two. He was in excellent health, active, and disciplined about his diet and exercise. But while he didn't expect to die at a young age, he did work intentionally to create a legacy for his children and his children's children.

In his last years on earth, Tom devoted himself to the study of God's Word and the application of that Word to his life. He was absolutely determined to be the husband and father God wanted him to be. As a result, he left Jennifer, Tommy, and me with an incredible inheritance—a legacy—of faith, love, and obedience to God.

That legacy has been a constant source of strength and encouragement for the three of us. Even now it continues to bless us. Hopefully it is a legacy that will be passed down for generations to come.

As I write about Tom's legacy, my inclination is to paint only a positive picture. Tom really was an exceptional person—not just in my eyes but in the eyes of many people. He maintained integrity and excellence in just about everything he attempted to do.

But he was not perfect. Neither am I. In previous chapters you've read about some of our struggles. Those difficult times were real, and they were painful. Ultimately Tom and I were just like most couples, working through the good and the bad and growing stronger in the process.

I Remember

I can be a little headstrong and impulsive. In the early days of our marriage, I'd get upset when life didn't work out the way I'd planned. My expectations for myself were sometimes unrealistically high. Whatever I did—whether it was exercising, studying, or working—I wanted to be the best.

Tom helped me work through some of my unrealistic expectations by reminding me that I was only responsible to do my best.

"Just do the best you can with what you're given," he'd say.

Tom lived that philosophy every day. He had been given a lot, and he used it well. He was so disciplined about . . . *everything*. That's one of the reasons he was so successful as a pilot. His success depended on his ability to follow through with what he'd learned. Not only did he have to learn and carry out difficult flight maneuvers; he had to maintain a level of excellence over years of flying. And he did.

When Tom became a Christian, he applied that same determination and commitment to his study of the Bible. He'd read something in the Bible, and then we'd talk about how to incorporate the related principle into our marriage. Parenting, finances, attitudes between husbands and wives—whatever the subject, he'd immediately want to make the necessary changes to bring his life into line with the Scriptures.

The example he set has been invaluable to me as I've had to make decisions for our family without him. By watching Tom I learned to go to God's Word to find wisdom and direction for life. In this and so many other ways, his legacy continues. And I continue, too, creating a legacy of my own.

Friends Remember

Chris Hoag, who greatly influenced our move to New Hampshire, told me that he and Tom connected right away—a real spirit-to-spirit connection.

"I was excited to be talking to another pilot who was a Christian," Chris said. "I was already jumping ahead to the thought that this guy could end up being a good friend." Chris and his wife, Rebecca, did become good friends.

"I don't know if Tom knew how Christlike he was," Chris told me recently. "He was very humble. Most pilots like to talk about themselves, but Tom didn't. His aviation background was pretty extraordinary, but he never brought it up. I had to pry it out of him."

Rebecca told me about a day when she came home to find Chris and Tom sitting on little children's chairs, having a tea party with Olivia, Chris and Rebecca's three-year-old daughter.

"Between tea-party talk, the guys were talking theology," Rebecca laughed.

Two other friends, Jeff and Vickie Thornhill, remember Tom coming out of the house to greet people arriving for a Bible study.

"He'd be out the front door before we could get out of the car," Jeff told me. "He was so open and welcoming."

Jeff also remembers that Tom was very focused on his faith.

"I have a little bit of aviation background," Jeff continued, "and I would start to talk to Tom about light aviation stuff. He'd nod politely and come back with a theology question. He was reading systematic theology between flying trips."

Vickie remembers a time when she and Jeff went out to dinner with Tom and me and a few other couples. The women were talking about salads, but Tom had started the guys on yet another theology topic by asking about something he'd read in his systematic-theology book.

"He wanted his life to change. He wanted to be what God wanted him to be," Jeff said in summary. "Tom wasn't into superficiality and pleasantries; he went right to real-life issues. And, at the same time, he had a warm and generous spirit."

Heartwarming Letters

After 9/11 I received many letters from pilots who had flown with Tom in the navy or at American Airlines. Their written testimonies to his character were not only heartwarming for me, they are a wonderful gift I can pass down to our children. They can know that their dad was well thought of in every area of his life.

One of the letters I received was from one of Tom's former commanding officers, currently an admiral working at the Pentagon. He penned a wonderful testimonial about Tom's flying skills and professional accomplishments. He wrote, in part: "Tom's achievements mark him as a man of incredible integrity, whose loss for our nation is irreplaceable. His patriotism, dynamism, and selfless courage are exemplary and priceless.

Tom's passing is a terrible loss, leaving a great hole in the fabric of our nation. He will be sorely missed."

Another of Tom's former commanding officers wrote, "I personally feel that Tom's greatest asset was his warm and generous personality. Unselfish with his time, he was always ready to assist anyone at a moment's notice. Genuine and sincere, he was strong in his beliefs and firm in his convictions. Without exception he always conducted himself as an officer and gentlemen in every respect. He will continue to be a source of admiration and respect for all who ever had the wonderful opportunity to know him. I feel without reservation that Tom was undoubtedly one of the finest officers I have ever served with in my twenty-four-year navy career."

Another close friend who flew with Tom in the navy wrote about the last time he'd had lunch with Tom in Boston before September 11. He remembered they had talked about so many things. "But as we talked that day in Boston, we drifted into a conversation about God and our purpose, and Tom said that he thought that in this life God is not so much concerned with our happiness, but with our faithfulness. Then he said he felt amazed (I thought he seemed almost embarrassed) that he was so very blessed and so very happy. To me Tom's legacy is one of achieving . . . faithfulness. Faithfulness to his country and his profession. Faithfulness to the church, his wife, children, family, and friends. And in all and through all, faithfulness to God."

The impact of these letters on my heart is almost overwhelming. Tom's legacy extends far beyond me and our children. The fact that he allowed himself to be used by God to touch so many lives takes my breath away at times. We all leave a legacy; that realization challenges me to do all that I can so that others might see the Lord in me.

One of my strongest motivations today for living with godly intentionality is my desire to love, comfort, teach, and train my children, as well as to build a life that leaves a legacy for them and for others that will go on after I am called home. Admittedly, in earlier years the thought of leaving a legacy was far from my mind. Like most people, I was so consumed with the moment that I didn't stop to think about the lasting impression my life would have. I am now aware of that impact, especially as I watch my children integrate Tom's beliefs into their own lives.

THESE COMMANDMENTS THAT I GIVE YOU TODAY ARE TO BE UPON YOUR HEARTS. IMPRESS THEM ON YOUR CHILDREN. TALK ABOUT THEM WHEN YOU SIT AT HOME AND WHEN YOU WALK ALONG THE ROAD, WHEN YOU LIE DOWN AND WHEN YOU GET UP.

—DEUTERONOMY 6:6–7

LOOKING AT THE PRINCIPLE

GOD DESIGNED YOUR LIFE

TO HAVE AN IMPACT ON ETERNITY.

1. We determine what our legacy will be.

When we leave our earthly lives, a part of us remains behind. That's our legacy: the impact and impression we made on others while we lived among them. Our legacy is the combined result of what we did and said in our lifetimes, the product of all the interactions we had with others. It is what we pass down to our children, our friends, and work associates, and everyone else with whom we had contact.

Each of us is responsible for our own legacy. We each determine what our legacy will be. And that legacy will be as positive or as negative as we choose to make it. The more conscious we are of our witness to others, the more opportunities we will have to create a legacy that draws others closer to God.

2. We are being watched.

Those of us who are parents know the feeling of being watched. With children in the house, it can sometimes feel as if we're living our lives under a microscope. Day by day, moment by moment, we have to be careful to live out what we say we believe. Little eyes are watching, and they're taking everything in.

Perhaps, like me, you have had the experience of seeing a trait of yours repeated in one of your children. You may have cringed a bit at the recognition. Or maybe you've heard words or phrases repeated by your child that you know he or she heard from you first. Children model what they see and hear from Mom and Dad.

Maybe you have been taken to task by one of those penetrating questions asked with childlike faith and innocence: "Gee, Mom, why did you cut that person off in traffic?" as you rush from school to baseball practice. Or, "Dad, can't we do something to help him?" as you move quickly by the homeless person sleeping on a park bench.

We need to work tirelessly to make sure our actions are consistent with our words and beliefs—that our private reality is the same as our public persona. We need to do this for our children's sakes. We also need to do it for the sake of others. Our children aren't the only ones who are watching.

Many people level the criticism that Christians are

hypocritical. Unfortunately, sometimes they're right. As believers, we are in the spotlight. Our actions are constantly being evaluated by onlookers, our words measured by how we live our lives. Is our behavior consistent with what we say we believe?

Ephesians 4:1 calls us to live with consistency: "As a prisoner for the Lord, then, I urge you to live a life worthy of the calling you have received." How do we do this? Fortunately, the Bible is full of instruction. Sometimes we view God's commands as a great, big "thou shalt not" list. But God wants us to live according to his Word, not out of guilt or fear or to keep up appearances, but because we love him and are grateful for the gift of his Son. He wants our hearts to be in line with our actions.

Ultimately, godly consistency begins in our thought life. Hypocrites are people who say one thing but think, and therefore do, another. Paul tells us: "Finally, brothers, whatever is true, whatever is noble, whatever is right, whatever is pure, whatever is lovely, whatever is admirable—if anything is excellent or praiseworthy—think about such things. Whatever you have learned or received or heard from me, or seen in me—put it into practice. And the God of peace will be with you" (Philippians 4:8–9). Thinking about these kinds of things will lead to actions that are consistent with what we say and believe—and to a positive legacy that will lead those who are watching us to eternal life in Christ.

3. Sometimes we need healing from past hurts in order to leave a positive legacy.

We all receive a legacy from our family of origin. For some this legacy is positive; for others it is not. If you were raised in a loving, godly family, you are fortunate and blessed. I encourage you to follow that example with your own family—to pass on the legacy. If, on the other hand, you grew up in a home environment or encountered circumstances that damaged your mind, body, or spirit, I encourage you to seek the help you need for healing. Only then will you be able to create a different, more positive legacy for those who follow after you.

The first step toward healing is to recognize that God loves you as a unique and precious individual. Of course, for many of us, believing that God really loves us as much as his Word says he does is not that easy. We mouth the words, "I know he sent his only Son to die for me," but our minds harbor a vast reservoir of old, negative words and experiences left over from childhood.

Thankfully those images from the past don't have to stay with us. They don't have to be a continuing influence on our present and our future. They can be replaced with new images that convey a new understanding of God.

As you know, Tom and I both had religious upbringings. What I remember most, though, are lots of rules, lots of "shoulds" and "should nots." Only when I entered into a personal relationship with Jesus did I really learn about God's great love for me. That's when I learned that I am important to him and that he has a plan for my life. This new understanding of God allowed me to replace some of the images from my past with a more positive image of God.

Tom did much the same thing. After coming to Christ, he took what he learned from Scripture and made it part of his life. He worked diligently, tirelessly, to learn more about God and what God wanted for his life. Then Tom taught these things to us. Others, too, learned from watching his example.

Jesus said, "If you hold to my teaching, you are really my disciples. Then you will know the truth, and the truth will set you free" (John 8:31–32). The great truth of the gospel is that Jesus loves you so much that he died for you. He paid the penalty for your sins. Inviting him into your life and living according to his teaching can set you free—free from the power of sin and free from the hurts you have experienced in the past.

Paul told the Philippian church, "I want to know Christ and

the power of his resurrection" (Philippians 3:10). That phrase, "the power of his resurrection," refers to the power that raised Christ from the dead—power that is fully capable of overcoming any hurt you've experienced, however deep or debilitating. I can honestly say it is the power of Christ's resurrection that has continued to help me overcome the pain and horror of 9/11. As I've discovered, that power isn't acquired by flipping a switch, like turning on an electric light. Rather, it is slowly integrated into my being as a result of deep, searching time spent with Christ.

Sometimes we need the help of others in the healing process. Depending upon the type and depth of hurt you've suffered, you may need to seek professional help. That's OK. One of the best ways to find a good therapist or counselor is to get referrals from friends. If you don't know anyone to ask, check with a pastor in your church. Some pastors have specific training as counselors, but many do not. Ask for a reference for a licensed counselor.

A Christian counselor can help you move from debilitation to healing. He or she can help you apply Scripture so that you come to understand how much God loves you and how to appropriate his resurrection power. The important thing to remember is that help is available. Don't wait. Once you have experienced significant healing, you'll be able to build a healthy legacy of your own that will have a positive impact on your family and others around you.

4. We can begin today to build a legacy.

You may be reading this and thinking, *You don't know how bad my past is. I've blown any opportunity I may have had to leave a positive legacy.* You're right. I don't know your past. But God does, and he can and will forgive you. (We'll talk more about forgiveness in chapter 11.) Not only will he forgive, but he will restore. As God says in Joel 2:25, "I will repay you for the years the locusts have eaten."

God spoke these words after calling the wayward Israelites to come back to him: "'Even now,' declares the LORD, 'return to me with all your heart, with fasting and weeping and mourning.' Rend your heart and not your garments. Return to the LORD your God, for he is gracious and compassionate, slow to anger and abounding in love" (Joel 2:12–13).

God always forgives and restores his people when they return to him. He will do the same for you. You can begin right now to live according to God's commandments and build a positive, lasting legacy. It's never too late. The consequences from your mistakes are a reality, but God is ready and willing to come into your life and begin to heal the damage. He will enable you to live in a way that will have a positive impact on the lives of others. What the locusts destroyed can and will be restored to wholeness. Decide to begin today.

Maybe you don't have a history of past, lingering hurts. Maybe you have lived a pretty good life for many years. But now you are aware that you are doing more than just living; you're building a legacy, an inheritance, for others, and you want to do that with more intentionality.

You, too, can decide to begin today. Focus on studying the Bible, which is God's instruction book for his people. Consider going to adult Sunday school, joining a Bible study, or just reading and studying on your own. Then apply the truths of Scripture that you learn, and pass them along to your family and others in your circle of influence. Begin today to build the kind of legacy that will draw other people to the love, forgiveness, and restoration of God—and impact eternity.

It's important to me that my children sense that we are still a family. With God's grace, our family of three is still a family—a complete family. And I am still a mom.

Chapter Seven

WHEN LOSS TOUCHES CHILDREN

Principle 7

GOD WANTS YOU TO APPROACH HIM AS YOUR HEAVENLY FATHER.

The pain reflected in my children's eyes pierces my very soul. My own loss is magnified many times over when I comprehend the loss my children will carry with them for the rest of their lives. Tragedy interrupted their tender teenage years and ripped away the most significant human being in their lives.

Tom was their defender, supporter, provider, encourager— their loving father in every way. His absence has created a hollow, hurting spot in their hearts that only Jesus can heal and fill. And he is doing just that. Jennifer and Tommy are healing and moving forward in the midst of their pain.

God is everyone's Father, of course. But I'm grateful that his Word makes special mention of his benevolence toward children who have lost their earthly father. According to Psalm 68:5, "a father to the fatherless, a defender of widows, is God in his holy dwelling." Today Jennifer, Tommy, and I are a strong three-person family. God answered my prayer that night of September 11: "Please don't let my children turn away from you, Lord." Jennifer and Tommy have remained faithful to God and are growing in their knowledge of him. They are young adults now. But they still struggle with the reality of life without Tom.

Jennifer's Story

I'll let Jennifer tell you some of her story in her own words:

"I wasn't a bookworm kind of student. I was more into fun activities and socializing. Dad put a lot of time into helping me with my schoolwork, teaching me in ways that meant something to me.

"Every night we would sit and do homework for about an hour or two. I needed the extra reinforcement of going over the lessons of each school day. Dad would read through my notes with me and re-explain them. He was my own personal tutor. When my report card would come out, he'd say, 'Let's see how *we* did.' It was a team effort.

"The night before a test, he'd spend even more time helping me go over the material; then we'd get up around 5:00 A.M. and go to Dunkin' Donuts. It would still be dark outside, and sometimes it was snowing. He'd even let me drive on those mornings and instruct me how to drive in the snow. (It was a short drive, and nobody else was on the road.)

"We'd do schoolwork in the restaurant until about 7:00 A.M. If we finished early, we'd just sit and talk about other things, mostly boys. My dad was very protective of my mom and me. He was a true gentleman, and he expected the boys around me to treat me the same way. If he heard a boy say something disrespectful, he'd have a little talk with him.

"I remember the way Dad would create teaching experiences. For example, he and Mom made up 'Caught You Being Good' coupons. If Tommy or I gathered a certain number, we got a prize. That made it fun to try to do what our parents wanted us to do.

"On Christmas Eve we would always exchange what Dad called 'gifts from the heart.' Usually these were gifts that we'd made. The point was for them to have special meaning. Before Tommy and I would open our special gifts from our parents, Dad and Mom would explain their meaning. When we were young, we didn't appreciate the talking as much as we did when we were older. We just wanted to open the gift!

"The gifts were never big deals materially, but we came to treasure them. One year Mom talked about a gift for me that reminded her of how I was growing into a lovely young lady. She said a lot of nice things that made me feel good about myself. Then I opened the package and discovered a beautiful porcelain holder filled with potpourri. I had been talking about wanting something just like it. Mom turned it into something that meant so much more.

"Next Dad handed me a box and started talking about me staying fit and doing my best all the time. He was a health nut, so we were used to his talks about eating well. I wasn't sure where his explanation was going, but his gift turned out to be a new leotard for gymnastics. It had black and white stripes with little stars all over it—really cute. (The leotard left our house, though, when a friend of Tommy's borrowed it. She didn't have a bathing suit, and they were going swimming. I never saw it again.)

"One evening I love to remember is the night I took a purity pledge at our church. It was really significant to me to make this commitment to stay pure until marriage, to do it in a public ceremony, and to have my parents involved. Before the event, Mom and Dad and I went and picked out a purity ring that I have worn constantly since that night. It's a simple yet beautiful band with little diamonds in it.

"During the ceremony I was so excited that I almost forgot to repeat the words of the pledge after the pastor spoke them. I was standing between Mom and Dad and just looking up at Dad with his big smile.

"'Are you going to say the pledge, Jen, or just take the ring?' Dad said with a grin.

"We all laughed as I hurried to catch up with what the pastor was saying.

"Of course, September 11, 2001, changed everything.

"Tommy and I were at school, and we had heard that there were two planes that had crashed into the World Trade Center. At first I didn't worry about my dad; I just felt terrible for all the families that had loved ones in the towers. Tommy and I go to a Christian school, so we began praying for those families, not knowing that our own family was in need of those prayers too.

"As I prayed, though, I had a picture in my mind of me walking down a church aisle. It was my wedding, and I was walking alone. Dad and I had talked before about him giving me away—walking his 'princess' down the aisle on her wedding day—so the picture seemed odd.

"Then our principal came into the room and called me out. As he walked with me to his office, I knew. I bit my lip and tried not to cry. My mom was in the office. She wasn't crying when I came in, but she looked like she was trying hard to be strong.

"'Jesus called Daddy home,' she said as she hugged me.

"If you ever have to tell your children that awful news, those are the most comforting words you can use. The way Mom put it, it wasn't just that Dad wasn't here anymore; he was in a wonderful place where we'd see him again one day. I had a picture of Jesus carrying my dad and cradling him into heaven.

"I have no regrets about my relationship with my dad. He was my best friend. I was his little girl. We'd have long conversations out on the deck; other times we'd walk around the neighborhood with my dog. He hadn't wanted a dog, but I won out on that one. Princesses always do.

"Since 9/11 my mom has become my inspiration. She's overcome so much and has become so strong. It seems like she is always doing something for other people, for Tommy and me, or for the ministry that God is giving her.

"I usually call her at lunchtime to check in with her. I want to be sure she's happy and has someone to talk to and that her day is going OK. Sometimes I need to talk to her to get moral support myself. We lean on each other.

"Once I went with my mother when she was speaking to a group. I was amazed to see her communicate so clearly about the love of God and the way he has helped us get through this time. The audience was so supportive and interested. They wanted to hear how God was working in our lives.

"I see that as a good thing that has come out of a terrible tragedy. God's gift to us has been to keep us going, to move us forward as his children, and to give us opportunities to tell others about him. It's exciting."

Tommy's Story

Now it's Tommy's turn:

"Three of my favorite memories of my dad are of going to Dunkin' Donuts, playing Ping-Pong, and playing baseball. When we'd go to Dunkin' Donuts, Dad would order a large, black coffee and a toasted, cinnamon-raisin bagel with strawberry jelly. If they didn't have strawberry, he'd order raspberry. I'd get a medium hot chocolate with whipped cream and a coffee roll.

"Most of the time we'd go over Scripture verses that I had to memorize for school. He'd have the verse in front of him, and I'd recite it. If I got it wrong, he'd give me back the paper and tell me to take a few more minutes to study it. Then he'd bite into his bagel and wait patiently. He didn't rush me or make me feel bad.

"I remember talking to him once about a difficulty I was having with a friend. This person had done some things to me that I didn't like, things that had hurt me. I couldn't understand why, since we had been friends for years. I'll always remember my dad telling me, 'Hurt people hurt people.' His words made me stop and think about what might have caused my friend to act the way he did. Dad always seemed to know the right things to say to help me understand about God and life.

"He bought me a Ping-Pong table for one of my birthdays, and we would play for hours. What I remember most, though, is the way Dad would talk with me while we played. I could talk with him about anything—school, girls, church, God, friends, *anything*. He would listen patiently and ask questions that would make me think. He seemed to use every opportunity to teach me something. He taught me a lot about sportsmanship, attitude, and humility.

"I think his favorite thing to do was to play baseball. He played baseball his whole life growing up—Little League, high school, and college. I never actually saw him play. But I think he must have been pretty good, because after he got out of high school and before he started college, he tried out with the Atlanta Braves.

"When we lived in California, it seemed as if we were out in the yard playing catch almost every night. I remember coming home from school one day and finding that my dad had built a pitching mound! Dad was a great coach, and he constantly encouraged me. We practiced together a lot. I will always remember him coming to my games and shouting from the sidelines, 'Throw strikes, buddy,' whenever I was pitching.

Even when I didn't have a very good game, he was always there to support me.

"We always had wonderful vacations together. I remember being in Hawaii and going out in the ocean with my dad. The waves seemed enormous to me. Dad would body surf into shore, and I'd be flapping around, unable to get in. Of course, the water wasn't really deep or dangerous; it just seemed that way because I was young. Dad would always come back quickly to help me, encouraging me to swim in by myself and cheering me on.

"I know I wasn't any more important than anyone else, but Dad always made me feel like I was the most important person in the world. Every day he told me he was proud of me and that he loved me.

"When I was about seven or eight years old, he took me on a flight that he was piloting. After takeoff he came back and sat with me. It was so cool. He explained to me about takeoffs and landings, the basic structure of airplanes, and other details about flying. Ever since that flight, I've wanted to be a pilot. Dad and I would talk about this dream for the future, when I would be his first officer, flying a jet; Jennifer would be a flight attendant; and Mom would be sitting in first class. A real family affair!

"Even after what happened on 9/11, I still want to be a pilot. Dad and I talked often about my future. I want to go to college, then flight school, and then join a branch of the service, the way my dad did. Of course, I want to get married someday and have a family too—a little Tommy to keep the line going.

"The toughest thing about Dad being gone is . . . *everything*. We did a lot together, and he was teaching me so many things. Just before September 11, we were starting to work around the house together. We were cleaning up the woods out back, and he was teaching me about the systems in the house.

"Those lessons have been helpful, because I'm the 'man of the house' now. I didn't like having people call me that at first. But I can see that in a way, it's true.

"I wonder what's going to happen to Mom when I go to college or move away. I don't think I'll live here all my life, but I do worry about Mom. Right now she seems fine, but what will her life be like when Jennifer and I are grown up? I feel responsible for that time in her life.

"Over these past few years, we've had many great friends who have been really nice to us. We get a lot of support from a lot of people. But we've also had to learn to rely on God, and because of that, my faith has grown."

I Am Still a Mom

In the early days after my loss, I had difficulty wrapping my mind around everything I needed to do now that I was head of the household. The vacuum created by Tom's absence was huge, and our family was floundering without his leadership. I knew that somehow I had to take on new responsibilities and step into the vacuum.

I prayed fervently that the Lord would show me how to do that—that he would show me what needed to be done on a practical level and on an emotional level to meet the needs of my family. We received so much help from our family and friends, and that made a big difference. But I knew I couldn't just sit around and let other people make decisions for us.

I felt physically exhausted and unsure of my ability to go from being the wife of a strong family man to being a single woman with a family. The task seemed daunting. But the Lord answered my prayers, and eventually Jennifer, Tommy, and I began to function as a family unit again. Over and over God showed me that in him I had strength I never knew I had.

We all cried a lot in those early days and weeks. I'd been advised to cry openly in front of the children, and I did that for a while. Then I realized that my tears upset them even more. They'd shift their focus from their own grief to mine and want to take care of me. So I stopped crying in front of them. They knew I still cried, but I don't think they felt as responsible for my feelings when I wasn't breaking down in front of them.

Jennifer struggled with staying in school. Classes had only

been under way for a few weeks when 9/11 happened. Afterward she didn't want to go back. Teachers and friends helped a lot. They were very caring and understanding. If Jennifer had to leave a class, no one made a fuss. She'd call me and we'd talk, and then she'd go back to class. My advice to her was to take it one class at a time, one moment at a time.

Nights were particularly rough for all of us. There is something about the quiet and darkness of night that draws the pain of our souls up to the surface.

One particular night Jennifer came into my room crying. "I need you, Mom," she sobbed. Then she crawled into bed with me, and I just held her.

The next day she told me what had upset her so much. She'd had a dream that Tom was alive. In the dream he called her on her cell phone and said he was in New York. He explained that he'd jumped out of the plane before it hit the tower and was OK. Jennifer jumped up and down and screamed for joy at the news—and that was all she could remember. She woke up to the cold reality that Tom was not in New York. He'd been called home.

I can only imagine what battles go on in the minds of my children as they grasp the ongoing reality of life without their dad. Sometimes I feel overwhelmed and unsure of how to help them. I have to remind myself to take one step at a time. *Lean on the Lord,* I tell myself, *and take the next step.*

It's important to me that my children sense that we are still a family. Yes, the structure has changed. We are no longer a family of four. But with God's grace, our family of three is still a family—a complete family. And I am still a mom.

Helping Children Deal with Loss

Many people ask me, "What advice do you have for parents who are helping their children deal with loss?" Of course, my own experience involves the death of my children's father. But most of what I've learned can apply to other kinds of losses too. Here are four points:

1. *Take care of yourself.* I've learned that I can't give what I don't have. If I'm physically exhausted, emotionally spent, and spiritually drained, I can't be of any help to my children. But where does a single mom find the time to take care of herself? That's the question I struggle with as I try to balance the speaking requests I receive with the needs of my kids. I feel called to take advantage of the opportunities that God is giving me to share my story. And of course, I need to provide financially for our family. At the same time, I need to be present for my children.

I've learned to ask questions such as, "Do I really need to do this?" "Can I drop this activity?" "How can I slow down and enjoy this day?" "When can I schedule a physical with my doctor?" "When can I get some time away with the Lord?" The answers to these questions have required some creativity on my part and a willingness to think outside the box and change the way I've been doing things.

I've had to be deliberate about plugging time into my schedule just for me. I used to think that doing something meaningful and nurturing for myself required setting aside a big chunk of time. Now I know that even a little time to myself is helpful. An hour sitting in a beautiful spot with nothing to do but rest is wonderful. So is taking a walk on the beach or soaking in a bubble bath. And this may sound like an old song, but I've found it helpful to get back to the basics of eating well and exercising. I'm back to working out most mornings, and I feel much better for it.

2. *Balance your own needs with the needs of your children.* There's a delicate balance between caring for yourself in a healthy way and caring for yourself in a way that neglects the needs of your children. As I learned with Jennifer and Tommy, their loss was as great as mine, and its impact was multiplied by their youth. They didn't have the resources of maturity I had to deal with the pain. They relied on me to be their source of strength and support.

That's why, in the early days after 9/11, I declined invitations to be a guest on various talk shows. I felt strongly that my children needed me to be at home with them more than I needed to be on television. They needed the security of my presence to help them adjust to a loss they could not understand.

3. *Teach your children to have an eternal perspective.* For children the loss of a parent is devastating. That's why it's vital for kids to understand the difference between physical death and eternal spiritual life. From the beginning I tried to teach Jennifer and Tommy to have an eternal perspective—the kind that looks beyond the grave and sees heaven. The loss of a loved one who knows Jesus is only a temporary loss! Tommy and Jennifer know they will see their dad again in heaven. Anticipating that reunion gives them great joy.

4. *Provide structure.* After a loss, life is chaotic. I know. Months go by with little thought of re-establishing a normal routine. Eventually any anticipation of a return to normal is replaced by the realization that your family will never again be normal the way it used to be. A new normal has to evolve.

As I began to heal from my grief and pain, I began to establish a new normal for Jennifer, Tommy, and me. Part of that new normal involved establishing new routines and a new structure for the family. I didn't try to replicate life as it used to be, but I did fondly incorporate the past in the context of an evolving present. I realized we were still a family—a new family with new challenges and new opportunities. The new routines and structure provided security for Jennifer and Tommy as they struggled to feel safe in their new world.

HOW GREAT IS THE LOVE THE FATHER HAS LAVISHED
ON US, THAT WE SHOULD BE CALLED CHILDREN OF
GOD! AND THAT IS WHAT WE ARE! . . . WE KNOW THAT
WHEN HE APPEARS, WE SHALL BE LIKE HIM, FOR WE
SHALL SEE HIM AS HE IS.

—1 JOHN 3:1–2

LOOKING AT THE PRINCIPLE

GOD WANTS YOU TO APPROACH HIM
AS YOUR HEAVENLY FATHER.

1. Our calling as parents doesn't change when we lose a spouse.

As parents we are called to love, train, and care for our children. The biblical imperatives are clear. And that responsibility doesn't go away when you lose a spouse; if anything, it increases in urgency. A single mom is still a mom. That doesn't change.

I am so thankful that I am the one God has called to lead Jennifer and Tommy. I consider it a privilege to be their mom. They are truly a gift. I love having the opportunity to teach them, guide them, and share this part of their life journey with them. God shows me daily how important my responsibility is toward them, and he constantly reassures me that I am not doing this alone; he is with me each step of the way.

2. The fatherhood of God is a spiritual reality.

Earlier in this chapter I quoted Psalm 68:5: "A father to the fatherless, a defender of widows, is God in his holy dwelling." What a promise! God himself is the one who will step in to fill the gap left by the absence of an earthly father and husband.

How does this work, though, when you're sitting at the table with bills piled up in front of you, the roof leaking over your head, and the kids asking for help with school? How does God provide what your husband used to provide?

For one thing, he uses other people to meet many needs. I have been able to teach my children so much about God's provision through others since September 11. Time and time again, God has stepped in and used the hands and feet of family, friends, and even strangers to provide for us in times of need.

But there are some needs that other people can't meet, such as the deep, aching need to experience the love and care of a father and husband. That need can only be met by the God of Psalm 68:5. As a spiritual father and husband, he provides help, protection, support, and love *spiritually*. It's a transfer that takes place from his heart to yours.

It is difficult to communicate the peace that flows through me when I completely rest in the arms of Jesus. Alone with

God—quiet, undisturbed, uninterrupted—I clear my mind of life's distractions and just talk with him. I feed my spirit with thoughts of his mercy, his goodness, his love. In moments of deep communion, I receive his indescribable gift of supernatural grace. I linger with him, then move back to the practicalities of life with new direction and energy.

Children can experience this kind of supernatural support too. Jennifer and Tommy have on numerous occasions. When you provide the environment for children to grow in the knowledge of Jesus, they can experience the blessing of his fatherly love in ways they can't even express.

3. God helps us with our parenting.

My biggest challenge today is launching my children into adult life. That's no different than the challenge all parents face; I just face it alone. Parenting is a huge responsibility, even when there are two adults to carry the load. When there is only one, the task can seem overwhelming.

I'm so grateful that Tom and I created a good foundation for our children. As a single mom, I've continued to build on that foundation, using the same beliefs and principles. Often, when parenting issues arise, I ask myself, "What would Tom do?" Sometimes I know the answer to that question; other times I don't, and I have to make the best possible decision on my own.

I approach parenting decisions just as I would any other: identify the situation, read what the Bible has to say about it, pray, seek wise counsel, then decide. It's certainly not the same as sitting down with Tom and discussing what to do about a particular parenting issue; but as time passes, I grow increasingly confident in my ability to sense God's will. Yes, I make mistakes. But more and more, with God's help, I'm learning to make good decisions.

Thankfully God promises in James 1:5, "If any of you lacks wisdom, he should ask God, who gives generously to all without finding fault, and it will be given to him." Often that wisdom comes from other men and women who are mature in the Lord. When I am uncertain about an issue having to do with my kids, I don't hesitate to find someone who has successfully raised children and ask for their advice.

4. We are loved by God more than we're loved by anyone else.

It's difficult for me to believe that God loves my children more than I do or more than Tom did. But he does. He loves each of us more than any human being ever could. That's why I want to grow to know my heavenly Father more and more: so I can be increasingly aware of his miraculous love and point my children to the one who loves them most.

One of my favorite passages about God's love is found in Ephesians 3:16–19. It's my prayer for Jennifer and Tommy: "I pray that out of his glorious riches he may strengthen you with power through his Spirit in your inner being, so that Christ may dwell in your hearts through faith. And I pray that you, being rooted and established in love, may have power, together with all the saints, to grasp how wide and long and high and deep is the love of Christ, and to know this love that surpasses knowledge—that you may be filled to the measure of all the fullness of God."

True godly parents lavish their children with love. But even the godliest human parents are limited in the love they can give. God, however, is not limited. He *is* love. And in his great love, he promises eternal life in paradise for those who trust in his Son, Jesus. The Bible says, "No eye has seen, no ear has heard, no mind has conceived what God has prepared for those who love him" (1 Corinthians 2:9). What a glorious hope we have when we respond in love to the amazing love of God!

After 9/11, my heart felt as if it were ashes. Over time, however, I realized that God was turning those ashes into something beautiful.

Chapter Eight

God's Calm in the Midst of the Whirlwind

Principle 8

God gives you new life as you step out to serve him.

Media requests came in immediately. In fact, the phone rang constantly those first few months after 9/11. Everyone, it seemed, wanted to interview me—television shows, magazines, radio programs. Initially I turned all of them down. I was too consumed with my own grief and with taking care of my children to think about such things. Gradually, however, I began to consider doing some interviews. God was moving in my heart, and I felt an urging to go ahead and speak out about how he was helping us.

One of the first shows I did was for a local television station about six weeks after 9/11. When the station called, I said that I would do the interview only if I could talk about God. I'd heard that the media in general won't let you talk openly about your religious faith, so I wanted to be sure to clarify this point. The station agreed to my condition. From that point on, that stipulation became my criteria for choosing which interviews I would and would not do.

My experience with the media has been very positive. People in the industry have been respectful, and they've been willing to accommodate my request that the final, edited versions of my interviews include my comments about my faith in God.

A New Purpose

Before 9/11, I had never been a public speaker. The very thought of speaking before a large group frightened me. When I spoke at Tom's memorial service, I put aside my fear for that one day, figuring I'd been given a once-in-a-lifetime opportunity to testify to the power of God in Tom's life. I didn't expect to speak in public ever again.

To my amazement God used my testimony at the service to touch lives. One Sunday morning at church, a man stood up and explained that he was one of the pilots who had attended Tom's memorial service. He told the congregation that he had expected the service to be sad and was surprised that it wasn't.

As he listened that day to what Tommy and I shared, his heart burst with emotion. He sat in the pew, sobbing. He wanted to escape, but getting out of the middle of the packed row without drawing a lot of attention to himself was impossible. In the end he asked Jesus to come into his life.

I spoke to this pilot after the church service and thanked him for the blessing his words were to me. I went home full. I could see that God's hand had worked through me, and I was excited.

A few months after the memorial service, I was asked to speak at church again. With much trepidation, I agreed. Afterward, a man in the congregation asked me to speak at a business convention.

"I don't do public speaking," I told him.

"What you said here today will be fine," he responded with a pleasant smile.

And so began a public-speaking ministry that continues to this day. In those early weeks and months after Tom's death, I couldn't imagine going on living. I thought my purpose in life had plunged to the ground with the World Trade Center. But I was wrong. As I began stepping out in faith, God showed me that he was powerful enough to carry me and the children—and not only carry us, but open doors for us to reach out to others. One of my favorite verses is Isaiah 46:4: "I am he who will sustain you. I have made you and I will carry you." I realized God was doing exactly that. And in the process, a new purpose in life was unfolding before me.

To be honest, I was terrified at first. Speaking to groups, traveling, sharing my story—those things were way outside my comfort zone. I felt so inadequate. I knew that God would have to give me the words, because I had no idea how to go about preparing a speech. *Don't be fancy, Cheryl*, I'd tell myself. *Just talk about the Lord and his care for you and the children.*

Up from the Ashes

It's a biblical truth that we give to others that which we have received. When we have suffered and received God's comfort, we want to pass that blessing of comfort along to others. I like the way Paul puts it: "Praise be to the God and Father of our Lord Jesus Christ, the Father of compassion and the God of all comfort, who comforts us in all our troubles, so that we can comfort those in any trouble with the comfort we ourselves have received from God" (2 Corinthians 1:3–4).

In earlier years I never would have believed that I could survive without Tom. Then the unthinkable happened—and I am surviving. The reason is God. In a supernatural way that is difficult to explain, God comes into the lives of his people who are hurting and restores them. His comfort doesn't remove pain; it heals in the midst of pain.

I know. My pain was all-consuming. Then Jesus, the Great Physician, came in and began to heal my troubled heart. Now I want to share the gift of comfort and hope that I received with other people who are hurting.

After 9/11, my heart felt as if it were in ashes. Over time, however, I realized that God was turning those ashes into something beautiful. And so the name of my ministry was born: Beauty Beyond the Ashes. The words come from Isaiah 61:3, in which God paints a beautiful picture of his restoring love: "[He has sent me to] provide for those who grieve in Zion—to bestow on them a crown of beauty instead of ashes, the oil of gladness instead of mourning, and a garment of praise instead of a spirit of despair. They will be called oaks of righteousness, a planting of the LORD for the display of his splendor."

Focused on Serving

Speaking (and now writing too) has given me a new focus in life. I left my career in human resources a year and a half before that fateful September day. Those months were full of joy. I loved being able to focus on being a mom and a supportive helpmate to Tom. I felt I was serving God by serving my family. But then those days ended. Now my focus is still on serving God—just in a different way. He's called me to a ministry that stretches beyond my immediate family. He has given me a story to tell, and he has brought hurting people into my life to listen.

When I first started speaking, I couldn't fathom how anything I might say could be of any help to anyone. But then I would talk to people after a speaking engagement, and they would tell me how much my words helped them deal with their own pain. I was constantly amazed.

I remember one couple who came up to me after a talk and told me about the grief they were going through because of the loss of their baby. Their precious little one had died just days before the mother's due date. How devastating! They said that what I shared that day had expressed exactly how they felt, only they hadn't been able to put it into words. They were blessed, and so was I.

The results of my speaking ministry regularly take my breath away. All I'm doing is opening my mouth and sharing what God is doing in my life. How could something so simple make such an impact? At times I ask, "Am I worthy to be doing God's work? Why would he choose me to serve him?" And then I receive cards, notes, or e-mail messages from people telling me that something I shared touched them at their very point of need—and my questions evaporate.

I don't feel worthy to be speaking in front of so many people, but I am grateful for the opportunities. The responses I receive feed me and bless me so much. They confirm to me that I am doing what God wants me to do. And they create a passion and excitement within me that keeps me going. Because I have this new purpose, I tend to do less looking back at *what was* and less looking ahead with painful feelings at what I don't have. Instead I do more focusing on *what can be* as I continue to move ahead, trusting and serving the Lord.

My personal mission statement includes three goals: (1) to stay focused on God, family, and relationships, and to love God and others; (2) to serve and not be served; and (3) to do the will of God. Establishing these guidelines has made it easier for me to make decisions about what to do and what not to do. They've also made it easier for me to check up on myself and make sure I'm staying on track. For example, if my family seems to be suffering because I'm on the road too much, then I know I have to slow down. If hearing God's whisper in the midst of the whirlwind gets to be too much of a struggle, then I know it's time to withdraw and be alone with God.

After all, everything I do in ministry is for his purposes and his glory. I'm not trying to "earn" God's favor or my salvation; that's impossible. God gives me eternal life as a free gift of his grace. At the same time, he does provide blessings for his faithful servants.

Jesus told a parable that illustrates the blessing we receive when we use the gifts and opportunities that God gives us to serve him. In the story a man was preparing to go on a journey and called his servants to him. He gave the first servant five talents of money. He gave the second servant two talents, and the third servant one talent. Then he left on his trip.

While he was gone, the first two servants used their talents. They invested them wisely and ended up multiplying them for their master. But the last servant buried his talent in the ground and had nothing more to show for it when the master returned. This last servant was reprimanded, but the first two servants got to hear these familiar words of Scripture: "Well done, good and faithful servant! You have been faithful with a few things; I will put you in charge of many things. Come and share your master's happiness!" (Matthew 25:21).

Sometimes I feel as if I have nothing to offer God—or anybody else for that matter. But God gives each of us gifts and opportunities that he wants us to use in service to him. And while the end result may not be glory, honor, and riches in forms that the world recognizes, God promises in his Word that he will give us these things as *spiritual* blessings if we will serve him faithfully out of hearts of gratitude and love. And one day we will have the amazing experience of standing before him and hearing those wonderful words: "Well done, good and faithful servant!"

WHOEVER SERVES ME MUST FOLLOW ME; AND WHERE I
AM, MY SERVANT ALSO WILL BE. MY FATHER WILL
HONOR THE ONE WHO SERVES ME.

—JOHN 12:26

LOOKING AT THE PRINCIPLE

GOD GIVES YOU NEW LIFE

AS YOU STEP OUT TO SERVE HIM.

1. All of us are called to serve. Service to God is part of the deal we get when we accept Christ.

It comes with our new life. The Bible addresses this point very clearly in James 2:14–17:

> What good is it, my brothers, if a man claims to have faith but has no deeds? Can such faith save him? Suppose a brother or sister is without clothes and daily food. If one of you says to him, "Go, I wish you well; keep warm and well fed," but does nothing about his physical needs, what good is it? In the same way, faith by itself, if it is not accompanied by action, is dead.

The "professionals" on the church staff aren't the only ones who are called to serve. The role of servant belongs to each and every one of us who claim the title of Christian. We may in fact be called to serve in some official capacity in a church or Christian organization. But more often than not, we are called to be unofficial servants, doing acts of service and blessing at home, at work, at church, and in the community as God directs our paths.

Whatever we do, service by definition must have a direct or indirect bearing on other people. A direct impact results from such service as visiting a shut-in or teaching a Sunday school class. A less obvious, indirect impact results from helping to paint the church building to make it more attractive, or packing boxes of food and clothing to send to missionaries overseas. Christ, whom the Bible says "did not come to be served, but to serve" (Matthew 20:28), is our role model. His service always had a very clear and personal relational element. We, too, must have a "people connection" somewhere in the process.

2. We can't serve well when we're exhausted or in deep pain.

It's true that we're all called to be servants. But sometimes we have to be grateful receivers first. After the shock of 9/11, it took time for me to heal and become strong enough to begin to think about giving to others. The needs of my family were so great that all I could do was cling to God's promises and thank him for his wonderful provision through the service of other people.

You, too, may be in a place of need. Perhaps you have experienced a deep personal loss, and your soul aches with a consuming intensity. Perhaps you are in the middle of a difficult, years-long situation that has drained you of your joy and well-being. Maybe you suffer from a physical condition that requires you to call on all of your physical, emotional, and spiritual reserves just to get through one day at a time. Maybe you are the mother of young children or the daughter of ill parents, and family demands are using up all the giving capacity you can muster.

You are not alone. All of us experience challenges in life at one time or another that leave us feeling empty and needy. We wonder, "How can I balance the need to spend time with my children and the need to spend time with friends and ministry partners? How can I balance the workload demands of ministry with the need for personal quiet time and physical, emotional, and spiritual renewal?"

If you are hurting or in need, I encourage you to find a place of rest and refreshment—either an actual, physical place where you can go to rejuvenate, or a mental state where your thoughts can go to the things of God that comfort you. Then rest there, secure in the knowledge that God will minister to you. Seek his healing. Seek his nourishment. When you have been refreshed, then you will be in a position to serve others more effectively.

3. Our attitude is to be like that of Jesus.

Paul describes Jesus this way in Philippians 2:6–11:

> Who, being in very nature God, did not consider equality
> with God something to be grasped, but made himself noth-
> ing, taking the very nature of a servant, being made in
> human likeness. And being found in appearance as a man,
> he humbled himself and became obedient to death—even
> death on a cross! Therefore God exalted him to the high-
> est place and gave him the name that is above every name,
> that at the name of Jesus every knee should bow, in heaven
> and on earth and under the earth, and every tongue con-
> fess that Jesus Christ is Lord, to the glory of God the
> Father.

Jesus denied himself to save us. As God's own Son, he
became our servant, suffering in our place on the cross. He also
became our example. Our calling as servants requires us to take
on the Christlike attitudes of willingness, humility, selfless giving, and joy.

Second Corinthians 9:7 says, "Each man should give what
he has decided in his heart to give, not reluctantly or under
compulsion, for God loves a cheerful giver." The principle of
cheerful giving applies to service too. God loves a cheerful servant! He wants our labor, our work, our service to be motivated

not by compulsion or guilt but by love, thankfulness, and a desire to do his good will.

If we give out of obligation instead of gratitude, we end up giving out of a dry well. Instead of being filled to overflowing ourselves, we become spiritually empty. This kind of service leads to frustration, disappointment, and resentment. We may sign up for a job and quit before our commitment is completed. Or we may press through to the end, but in a way that is anything but cheerful.

To be truly cheerful servants who are not drained by their efforts and who experience blessings in return, we need to examine our attitude before accepting new opportunities to serve. We need to measure our motives against the model of Christ. We need to ask, "Am I doing this with the heart of a servant? Is my attitude like that of Jesus?" It is an old but true adage that when God examines our work, he looks not at our hands but our heart. He doesn't look at our results; he looks at our attitude.

4. God works through each of us in unique ways.

We are all created in God's image, but that doesn't mean we are all the same. Obviously, each of us has a unique set of physical attributes. Each of us has a unique set of skills, gifts, and talents as well.

The trouble is, we often fail to appreciate our uniqueness and instead try to gauge our value and worth by comparing ourselves with others. But the Bible clearly states that we are all unique parts of one body, and each part is important:

> The eye cannot say to the hand, "I don't need you!" And the head cannot say to the feet, "I don't need you!" On the contrary, those parts of the body that seem to be weaker are indispensable, and the parts that we think are less honorable we treat with special honor. And the parts that are unpresentable are treated with special modesty, while our presentable parts need no special treatment. But God has combined the members of the body and has given greater honor to the parts that lacked it, so that there should be no division in the body, but that its parts should have equal concern for each other. If one part suffers, every part suffers with it; if one part is honored, every part rejoices with it. (1 Corinthians 12:21–26)

How do you find your place of service? How do you know if you're an eye or a hand or a foot in the body of Christ? The more time you spend with the Lord asking him to reveal to you how and where he wants you to serve, the clearer it will become. You will begin to hear him whisper, "Say yes to this opportunity," or, "Say no to that invitation." Remain faithful, and he will unfold his purpose for you. And remember: The way you serve God today may change as your life situation changes. The key is to stay close to God, be sensitive to his calling, respond with the right attitude, and trust him for the result.

The truth is, we can experience God's blessing even as we experience pain, temptation, and loss that are part and parcel of life here on earth.

Chapter Nine

MIXED BLESSINGS

Principle 9

GOD PROMISES YOU HIS PRESENCE,
NOT A TROUBLE-FREE EXISTENCE.

I used to look at people who got up to speak to large audiences about God's goodness and assume they didn't have any big problems in their lives. I figured God had touched them in the wake of some particular life experience and moved them up the spirituality scale. They had applied the truths of Scripture so effectively over the years that pain, fear, and tension of any kind were gone. I really never thought about their lives apart from their presence on the stage, where they looked so confident and secure. Surely they had paid their dues in life's Department of Difficulty and were now exempt from further struggle.

How wrong I was.

It's natural to draw conclusions about people based on what they say, what they write, how they carry themselves—as if we're seeing them in their entirety. But I understand now that all of us, no matter how confident we appear in certain situations, live with tension. That doesn't mean that speakers are being deceptive when they share how God has touched their lives with his love, goodness, and blessing. It just means that life this side of heaven remains a struggle; and in the midst of the struggle, there is God.

I find it tempting to write only about God's blessings, in hopes of honoring him and drawing others to him. My relationship with God through his Son, Jesus, is definitely the mainstay of my existence. Without God I would be nothing. The tragedy of 9/11 would have incapacitated me, left me completely unable to carry on as the leader of my family. With God's grace we are doing well.

But I wouldn't want to mislead and cause anyone to think that God's miraculous touch always means that pain is instantly over and all tension is gone. Sometimes the relief is immediate. Sometimes the process takes longer. If we think that accepting Christ and walking with him means a pain-free life, we will be disappointed. If, on the other hand, we understand that Christ comes in and supernaturally enables us to live through painful realities in the embrace of his love, we will receive a power that will amaze us.

I still can hardly believe that Jennifer, Tommy, and I are living well without Tom. The pain of loss is piercing, and yet we are living full lives and growing in ways that could only be possible with God's help.

Christians, like everyone else, have challenges. Life is full of them. But through all the challenges and uncertainties, God calls us to trust him. He calls us to step into the dark unknown by faith and allow him to light our way. Tommy, Jennifer, and I know that we're still on that journey. We are traveling a path marked by choices, decisions, and experiences, many of which are difficult and painful. But as we travel that path, in spite of the struggle, we are very aware of God's provision and blessing.

The truth is, we can experience God's blessing even as we experience the pain, temptation, and loss that are part and parcel of life on earth. I've found that by accepting this fact, I no longer have to strive to accomplish the impossible task of eliminating all the negatives of life; I can strive instead to know God and his power in the context of those negatives. I can acknowledge his power to carry me through difficulty without having to remove that difficulty. And as God's love lifts me above my pain, my heart can fill with joy. My soul can soar despite my circumstances.

Making Tough Decisions

In the early days after 9/11, I had lots of help making decisions. But as the days turned into weeks and months and then years, I had to assume the primary responsibility for our family. As I grew stronger, I was able to think more clearly and make wise choices. But it wasn't always easy.

A lot of well-meaning people asked, "Are you going to move?" "Can you afford to keep your house?" "Will your children stay in their Christian school?" "Will you go back to work?" "Are you OK financially?" "What are you going to do with the rest of your life?" I couldn't understand. These people had never asked me such things before. Why did they feel free to ask such personal questions now?

The intrusiveness of their inquiries created tension and turmoil inside me. I didn't want to be rude or hurt anyone's feelings, but I also didn't feel obligated to answer probing personal questions. However well intended, the questions were more anxiety producing than helpful. Over time I developed ways to avoid giving answers. Usually people got the message and dropped the subject.

Slowly I've gotten my feet planted in my new turf as chief

decision maker for my family. I feel that I am rising above the ashes with God's help. But I still struggle. My natural inclination is to have everything under control—to have all the details of life worked out ahead of time. This chafes against my inability to guarantee that every decision will work out the way I want it to.

Differing opinions confuse me. Should I buy nursing-home insurance or invest that money in hopes of earning enough to cover future healthcare costs? What if I never need to go into a nursing home? What should I do about house and car maintenance? Finances? College for the children? Ministry direction? Who will feed the dog when we travel? The decisions I face on any particular day can range from trivial to enormous.

One day I was sitting at my desk at home, preparing my thoughts for an upcoming speaking engagement. As I sat there thinking, a drop of water bonked me on the head. Then another drop fell, then another. Before I realized what was happening, plaster and moldy debris were raining down on me.

I called a plumber, and he discovered a leak in the bathtub in the bathroom above my office. The unknown leak had been gathering force for months, and the accumulation of water finally broke through.

What to do? This seemingly small matter initiated a whole cascade of decisions I'd never had to make before. In the past

Tom took care of everything to do with the house. Now all of those decisions are mine. My address book contains new listings: plumber, electrician, handyman.

Fortunately, my nature is to move on once I've made a decision. I generally don't dwell on a matter and second-guess myself. But when I'm feeling overwhelmed with the details of life, and the decisions I need to make are mounting up, my head can start to spin. My hands get cold and clammy, I feel disoriented, my breathing speeds up, and I start to sweat. These symptoms only last a few minutes, and then I usually call someone and talk through my feelings.

Keeping a manageable schedule helps to keep me from getting to that point. So does being honest about what I don't know. I've learned that I have to be willing to ask for help; if I try to figure out the answer to everything myself, the inner tension grows. It also helps that I have wonderful people around me to give me advice. If these friends and family members don't know about a particular issue, they refer me to someone who does.

Emotional Ups and Downs

People often ask me what they are doing wrong. "It's been awhile since my loss, and I'm still experiencing pain," they tell me. The fact is, they may not be doing anything wrong. After a loss it's normal to move back and forth between joy and sadness. That emotional roller coaster is not necessarily an indication of weakness or insufficient faith. It is part of the human condition. Your feelings will eventually even out. The depths of sadness are not so deep. Moments of despair are less frequent. Periods of peace and joy increase as you experience more and more of God's love, provision, and healing touch.

Looking back through my journal, I can see just how much my emotions have surged and dipped over these last few years. I've gone from low moments of complete despair to high moments of joy within a matter of days.

For example, on January 22, 2002, I wrote:

Lord, I know you understand my feelings. It is so painful. I don't feel I have the strength to carry on. I know you can heal my heart. You are my refuge and strength, but I don't feel I have the strength to even say those words. All I can do is think them and know that you hear them. I want this sadness to stop. I want my joy restored. When will you restore it? Please restore me, before I die.

Why did you call Tom home? I'm not strong enough to live in this world without him. I need him to care for me and love me.

Life isn't fun. The only joy I feel is when I bare my soul

for you. When I speak and words come out. Words about your strength, your power, your love. Lord, I am nothing but dust. I will blow away someday. Your Word lives on forever.

A month later, in February 2002, I wrote:

God is teaching me to walk by faith, not by sight. God has provided for my family in ways I never imagined. The body of Christ is faithful. God continues to strengthen my faith so I can be an encouragement to others. My eyes are open not only to the big stuff but to the small stuff. The power of the Holy Spirit is so present in my heart.

It took hitting rock bottom emotionally and crying out to God for me to begin to experience real healing. Now I know that when I pour my heart out to God in my journal or in my prayers, my emotional tension is released. That's why God wants us to be open and honest with him: When we admit our struggles, then he can come in and heal us.

Back to Work

It feels strange to consider my ministry "work." Speaking and writing are not things I previously studied or sought after. God opened these doors for me, and now I am walking through them.

Of course, it would be wonderful if ministry didn't have any of the tensions of other kinds of work, but it does. Still, the blessings of ministry outweigh the tensions. I meet wonderful people and receive such support and encouragement. I don't fully understand how telling my story helps others, but I see that it does. When people share pain, they can also share comfort and hope. The reality that God is helping my family means that he will help other families also. His love is available to all who believe in his Son.

I feel the tensions of ministry most when I am overly tired. Recently I went to a retreat as a participant, not a speaker. I knew what I really needed was rest and time alone at home, but I felt obligated to go. I'd been involved in the planning, and I wanted to support my friends who helped put the retreat together.

The problem was, I was giving from a dry well instead of from an overflow of God's provision. At the retreat, as we sat in small groups and talked, the subject turned to 9/11. Someone started to share about what happened that day at her children's school, and my overloaded system suddenly began to scream for attention. My head ached; my stomach was in knots; I was getting irritable. At the evening session, the topic of 9/11 came up again. The speaker said something about bodies being found huddled together. I could hardly stand it.

I managed to slip a note to the speaker, asking to meet with her. She was wonderful. She recognized my fatigue immediately and encouraged me to leave early and go home. Her words were so freeing. Immediately the tension began to drain out of me.

As I drove home, I listened to a tape of beautiful music that brought tears to my eyes. But the night sky was dark, and a dense fog was rolling in. Suddenly driving became a challenge. My fear grew, and the tension I'd felt earlier returned in full force. I gripped the steering wheel of my minivan and prayed aloud, "God, please get me home safely."

He did, and I went to bed praising him for his protection. In the morning I woke up with a grateful heart. I was glad to be alive, glad to be home, and glad that the tension of the night before was gone.

Demands of work, ministry, friendships, and family can cause all of us to push ourselves too hard at one time or another. I've learned that I need to continually check in with the Lord to make sure that I'm doing what he wants me to do—and not what I think is expected of me, whether those expectations are mine or others.

Spiritual Intimacy

One of the greatest tensions I've experienced since 9/11, one of the deepest pains, is loneliness. At times it seems as if the world is full of nothing but couples. In restaurants or movie theaters, at church, walking down the street: All I see are pairs.

When I was working in human resources and had to travel alone quite frequently, I never actually felt alone. I could go into a restaurant for a meal by myself and sit comfortably with a book or some paperwork. I knew that Tom was home with Jennifer and Tommy, and I would soon return to my loving family. Now when I go into a restaurant by myself, I sometimes feel as if I have a sign on my forehead that reads, "Alone."

I miss the long conversations Tom and I had all of our lives together. We shared so much and so often that I don't remember ever thinking about something and not discussing it with him. Now I have no special person to share with on that level or to that degree.

But does that really mean I'm alone? The answer, I've learned, is no. With God I am never alone.

Yes, some of my dreams were crushed on September 11, 2001—the dreams that were wrapped around my marriage, the dreams that Tom and I had talked about since I was sixteen. But slowly over the months, God has shown me a new way. He has called me to himself, into a relationship I never would have imagined possible. I used to think that I had to have a husband to be complete. I have come to realize, however, that's not necessarily true. I was created by God as a unique individual. He gave me the gift of life and made me who I am—gifts and talents, warts and all. I am his creation, and that makes me special. He loves me and has a plan for me, for my life. That plan may also involve someone else, but it may not. And whether or not it involves someone else is not as important as growing closer to God and becoming all that he wants me to be.

I am learning more each day. The circumstances of 9/11 have forced me to examine who I am, to face myself in ways that I never had to before, to ask, "What does God want for me? What can I do in him, by his power within me? How will he use me to touch others?" I am learning more about myself and about God. And I am learning it on my own, not through Tom's filter.

For so many years, I relied on Tom to show me, teach me, and lead me. That wasn't bad; in fact, in many ways it was very good. But I feel that sometimes that degree of dependence may not have been healthy for me. It fed my laziness. I have come to appreciate the value of a strong interdependence in relationships. What Tom and I had was very good, but I'm learning that it might have been even better. I was so reliant upon Tom that I may have neglected my own individual development.

It's important for husbands and wives to strengthen themselves and pursue their own spiritual growth in order to better serve God and one another. Being strong as individuals allows spouses to have a healthy balance of dependence and independence in their relationship. Each person is able to contribute more to the relationship, utilizing his or her respective strengths for the common good. And a safety net of strength is there in case the unexpected happens.

In my own spiritual walk, I have drawn closer to the Lord since Tom died. I have a new understanding of what Jesus means in his Word when he talks about the church as his bride. I have found joy as the bride of Christ. I have found joy with Christ, the lover of my soul.

My desire to draw closer to Christ has led me to do those things you would normally do to develop any relationship. I spend time in his Word to learn more about him. I talk with him daily in prayer. I share my joys, my sorrows, my experiences, and my trials with him. I talk about him with others. The closer I draw to him, the more I feel an overwhelming desire to be with him, to share my life with him, and to experience all that he has for me. And in that ever-deepening intimacy, he brings me fulfillment—a spiritual fulfillment that is far greater than anything I have known.

God is showing me day by day that he truly does love me, and he will meet all of my needs. He is teaching me that I can still experience joy, peace, and love in my life, even without Tom by my side.

THIS IS WHAT THE LORD SAYS TO YOU: "DO NOT BE
AFRAID OR DISCOURAGED BECAUSE OF THIS VAST ARMY.
FOR THE BATTLE IS NOT YOURS, BUT GOD'S."

—2 CHRONICLES 20:15

LOOKING AT THE PRINCIPLE

GOD PROMISES YOU HIS PRESENCE,

NOT A TROUBLE-FREE EXISTENCE.

1. Tension can indicate the need to evaluate pressure in our life.

The dictionary defines *tension* as "being stretched tight, strained, taut." Think of a rubber band. A rubber band is made to withstand a certain amount of strain. We stretch a rubber band around a bundle, confident that it will withstand the strain and keep the bundle tightly wrapped. But what happens if the bundle is too big, and we pull the rubber band beyond its stretching point? It snaps in two like a crisp carrot.

We human beings function in a similar way. We are created with the ability to sustain a certain amount of stress, pressure, and strain. This ability is necessary for survival in a fallen world, where no one is immune from life's challenges. Like a rubber band, we are able to stretch under the strain—but only so far.

After 9/11 I was physically and mentally exhausted. At

times I didn't know how I was going to take even the next step. It was all I could do some days to remind myself to breathe. I felt stretched to the snapping point. Then slowly the healing began. From those slow, tentative first steps, I eventually learned to walk again. And as I learned to walk, my calling evolved. God showed me how he wanted me to serve. He gave me opportunities to serve; but only as I healed, only as I was able.

God has given all of us the means to handle life's challenges without snapping like a too-tight rubber band. The first is prayer—crying out to the Lord with honesty and vulnerability. The second is talking with wise Christians to obtain godly counsel. The third is reading the Bible and meditating on God's words of truth. As we do each of these things, our ability to cope with the pressures of life is strengthened and we are able to function.

If you feel like a rubber band that's about to snap, it's time to evaluate the pressure in your life. Understand, the tension you feel is an indication of stress. Step back from the whirlwind and consider what is burdening you. If I don't do this from time to time, my world spins quickly out of control. When I feel over-stretched, I know I need to focus more on God. I need to draw closer to him. I need to set aside my selfish perspective and seek him first. The more I seek him, the more aware I am of his plentiful provision, and the more he meets all my needs.

You may only need a day away with the Lord to hear him whisper an answer to your dilemma. Rest, pray, listen. In the quiet of God's embrace, allow him to restore you. Life may not change from hectic to calm overnight, but you will have greater inner peace. And you'll have the strength and resolve to make the changes—sometimes just little changes—that will relieve the pressure.

2. Sometimes tension exists because we're afraid to do something we know God wants us to do.

Tension calmly puddles beneath the surface of our consciousness when life is good, relationships are peaceful, and we are performing familiar tasks that don't challenge our abilities. But what happens when trouble brews, relationships erupt, and we face a task that's way outside our comfort zone? Those puddles of tension simmer, bubble, and boil over. We become filled with fear: *I can't do this. I can't talk to that person. I can't, I can't, I can't.*

Moses had a similar problem when God told him to go to Pharaoh and challenge him to let the Israelites leave Egypt:

Moses said to the LORD, "O Lord, I have never been eloquent, neither in the past nor since you have spoken to your servant. I am slow of speech and tongue."

The LORD said to him, "Who gave man his mouth? Who

makes him deaf or mute? Who gives him sight or makes him blind? Is it not I, the LORD? Now go; I will help you speak and will teach you what to say."

But Moses said, "O Lord, please send someone else to do it." (Exodus 4:10–13)

Of course, Moses went on to obey God, confront Pharoah, and lead the Israelites out of Egyptian bondage. And just as he promised, God gave Moses the words and the courage he needed to accomplish the task. In the same way, when God calls us to serve outside of our comfort zone or beyond our previous experience, he gives us the ability to do the job. We just have to trust him and move forward.

If we resist his direction, tension and pressure churn within us. Contrary voices battle in our minds, and conflicting feelings wrestle in our spirits. But taking that first step in faith relieves the tension; taking another builds confidence; and taking one more fills us with God's peace.

3. Sometimes tension exists because we're tempted to do something we shouldn't do.

For Christians, wrestling with temptation always causes tension. We may think, *This isn't so bad. I can handle this temptation. God will understand.* But the Holy Spirit lives inside us. He is grieved when we dabble with sin. If we linger mentally, emotionally, or physically in the vicinity of temptation, our fleshly spirit comes into direct battle with the Holy Spirit, and tension boils.

First Corinthians 10:12–13 gives us good advice about temptation: "So, if you think you are standing firm, be careful that you don't fall! No temptation has seized you except what is common to man. And God is faithful; he will not let you be tempted beyond what you can bear. But when you are tempted, he will also provide a way out so that you can stand up under it."

Maybe you're thinking, *But I am being tempted beyond what I can bear.* Whenever we think a temptation is too difficult for us, we're wrong; we just missed the way of escape. God always provides a way out—but it's up to us to take it. If we don't, the temptation will grow stronger, and so will the tension.

4. God's Word promises, "I can do everything through him who gives me strength."

For many of us, it's hard to grasp the truth of Philippians 4:13. How could we possibly do "everything" through Christ? In order to fully understand the promise of this verse, we need to consider it both in its immediate context and in the larger context of the rest of the New Testament.

In the closing portion of his letter to the Philippians, Paul writes that he has learned to be content, whatever his circumstances. He has learned to trust God for provision; and because he's had the experience of seeing God meet his needs time and time again, he boldly states, "I can do everything through him who gives me strength." We, too, can claim this promise if we know, as Paul did, that we are in line with God's calling, and our requests measure up against the standard of his Word. When we have the assurance that we're in the center of God's will, then we can step out as Paul did, trusting God's Word that he will provide.

I have seen this principle play out in my own life so many times since September 11, 2001. Life's circumstances have forced me to turn to God for my strength time and time again. And whether the matter has been small (fixing a leaky pipe) or major (being an effective single parent), God has provided. He has shown me over and over again that he is with me. And through him—by the power and strength of his Holy Spirit—I can do things I never imagined I could do.

I gently hugged the paper and thought, *God has sent me a red rose. This is a love letter from God.*

Chapter Ten

GROWING AND HEALING

Principle 10
GOD USES LIFE'S EXPERIENCES
TO BRING HEALING IN TIME.

I wish we could all sleep through tomorrow morning and miss reliving the moment that Tom left us.

It was the night of September 10, 2002. With the dawn would come the one-year anniversary of 9/11. How I wanted to avoid the next morning! I purposely didn't set an alarm, but I knew the children and I would wake up before 8:46 A.M., the moment Tom's plane crashed into the World Trade Center.

We'd thought about going out for a nice breakfast, but I didn't want to be out in public when church bells started ringing all over town. To commemorate that fateful day, the city of

Portsmouth planned to ring bells at the exact time Tom's plane hit the tower. It was a nice gesture, but I didn't want to be sitting in a restaurant listening to a waitress or another customer say something that might make me break down and cry.

Our neighbors were so considerate. They asked me in advance what they could do on the anniversary. I told them I wanted to keep the day low-key.

"What if we bring over breakfast for you and the kids in the morning?" a few women offered.

"That sounds nice," I told them.

So as I climbed into bed—the same bed I'd slept in with Tom for the last time exactly one year before—I prayed: "God, help us get through tomorrow. Help Jennifer and Tommy to feel your presence. Help us."

I woke up around seven, long before the tolling of the bells. I put on a pot of coffee, called one of the neighbors to let her know I was up, and opened my front door to get the newspaper. I was greeted by a most beautiful sight: baskets of fall-colored mums lining my driveway. Quietly, respectfully, neighbors continued to arrive, placing even more flowers all the way down both sides of the long, winding path. Their gesture was both loving and low-key. My heart filled with gratitude.

The women who made breakfast delivered a feast: omelets, fresh fruit, Danish pastries, fresh orange juice. We decided to eat out on the deck, which was bathed in the warm glow of sunlight filtering through the trees. I shuddered, realizing that this was the very spot where I'd been sitting a year before, when the phone call came that changed my life forever.

But now, out in the sunlight with my children and wrapped in the love of neighbors, I felt relieved. My anxiety about the day was gone. It was a beautiful morning. Evidence of God's grace was flowing all around me. We did hear the town bells ring, but the moment passed quickly, and I was grateful that our day was off to a good start.

When we had first started talking about the approaching anniversary, Jennifer and Tommy had said that they didn't want to go to school that day. But by the time September 11, 2002, arrived, they had changed their minds.

"We live September 11 every day, but it is good for the world to commemorate the loss our nation experienced," I told them. We focused again on where Tom is—in heaven, with Jesus— and how blessed we are to know that we will see him again. Afterward, they agreed to go to school—but a little late so we could have a special breakfast together.

As we enjoyed the bountiful meal, we reminisced and talked about the last year of all our lives. It was a bittersweet time. We prayed together. Then I kissed my precious children and watched them drive off down the flower-lined driveway. *Thank you, God,* I prayed silently as they pulled away. *I have worried about this morning for so long, and we have made it through. The children are OK. Thank you, thank you!*

Later that day I participated in a tree-planting ceremony in front of the Portsmouth post office. I had the opportunity to thank the people of Portsmouth—this wonderful community that had so quickly become our home—for their outpouring of love and support. The tree was one of ten that were planted in New Hampshire communities where someone had died in the World Trade Center attacks. This one was in memory of Tom. It was a moving tribute.

The rest of the day was filled with routine events. I went to watch Seth, Jennifer's boyfriend, play soccer and then to watch Tommy run in a cross-country meet. Then it was evening, and we were off to church.

An overflow crowd was in attendance—more than fifteen hundred people. Television and radio crews were there, along with members of the press. My primary concern was for Jennifer and Tommy. I didn't want them to feel overwhelmed.

Before the service began, I had a quiet time in prayer with two close friends. I could almost feel God's hand on my shoulder as my anxiety dissipated. I was able to step confidently to the microphone and share the words that God gave me, the words that were on my heart—words about legacy, servanthood, and forgiveness. I told the audience how God had enabled us to march boldly forward. How we had not allowed ourselves to be given over to bitterness or fear. How I had resolved that the terrorists would not win the war for my heart—nor for the hearts of my children.

And then it was over. Surrounded by friends, I relaxed, knowing that I could go confidently forward now. God had seen us through the first year. He had been there during our moments of pain and our times of trial. But he had also given us many moments of triumph.

Difficult Dates

September 11, 2002, wasn't the only difficult date that we faced after 9/11. With Tom gone, regular holidays and special family events became a major challenge for me. I had always approached Christmas, Thanksgiving, birthdays, anniversaries, and family vacations with lots of energy, excitement, and emotion. After Tom died I realized it was important to continue to celebrate—for the well-being of Jennifer and Tommy and for my own healing. But I couldn't help but feel anxious about how these events were going to be planned and put together and what effect they would have on us when they were over.

Slowly God has given me the confidence to celebrate these special days again. He has shown me how to remake these events in ways that are positive and healthy without ignoring or denying what was. Still, it's been a struggle.

One of the most difficult days actually came a month before the one-year anniversary of 9/11. August 6 was our wedding anniversary—a date that Tom and I had always enjoyed celebrating. As the date approached, my anxiety level increased daily. I wasn't sure how I was going to feel. I wasn't sure what my emotions would do. I hoped futilely for a miracle that would cause the calendar to jump from August 5 to August 7.

Thankfully, Jennifer and Tommy stepped in. On August 6, 2002, they took me out to dinner. We were able to sit down and celebrate as a family. We looked back at the marriage Tom and I had enjoyed and shared happy memories.

"I know Dad's not here," Jennifer told me, "but I saw what you and Dad had, and I know I want that for myself."

Two other holidays not quite a year later became lessons in "how to" and "how not to" handle special events. I gave very little thought to Mother's Day 2003 as it approached. One of my friends suggested that Jennifer, Tommy, and I join a group of friends who were planning a get-together that day. Since I'd made no plans myself, I agreed to go along with the crowd. The kids and I joined the group at a local restaurant after church for brunch.

As we drove to the restaurant, the thought crossed my mind, *Why are we doing this?* Then, as we walked into the dining room and saw more than a dozen people seated around a large table, I knew: *This isn't what I want to do.* I wanted the day to be one that would focus on Jennifer and Tommy and how special they were to me. I wanted them to know that nothing made me happier than being their mother. I wanted to celebrate Mother's Day with them—alone. But here we were, swept up in an event that was carrying me off in one direction while my feelings and emotions raced off in another.

I couldn't make it through the meal. I crashed. One innocent comment or two about loss, about what no longer was, sent me off the deep end. Our friends were honestly and understandably confused. Their well-intentioned effort to include us in the party had gone awry. They had no idea what was going on inside me. The problem was me, not them. And my crash only reinforced the fear and anxiety about holidays that I had been working to overcome since 9/11.

The disaster of Mother's Day gave me the resolve I needed to take control of Father's Day the next month. I reassumed family leadership and planned an event that would focus on Jennifer and Tommy and the great dad they have. (I purposely use the word *have* rather than *had* when talking with the kids about their dad. I want them to appreciate that even though Tom isn't here with us physically, he is alive with God, and they still have a dad.)

On Father's Day 2003, the three of us came home after church and worked together to make a special meal. We had a great time in the kitchen, enjoying each other's company as we cooked. After dinner we spent several hours going through our collection of old family photographs. I had purchased a number of new photo albums, and we spent the evening sorting and organizing our family pictures. In the process we remembered in a positive and joyful way the many wonderful years we had with Tom as a husband and dad.

God's Love Letter to Me

One beautiful, sunny day about two weeks after the one-year anniversary of 9/11, my spirits weren't matching the weather. I was feeling low, and my heart was heavy. I decided to go for a walk along Rye Beach, a lovely area about ten minutes from my house, where I often go to walk, think, pray, and spend time with the Lord.

As I walked along the shoreline, watching the waves break leisurely over the rocky terrain, I began to pray: "Lord, you're my redeemer, you're my salvation, you're my hope, you're my love, you're my provider, you're my refuge, you're my strength, you're my Abba, you're my—" And for the very first time I said, "You're my husband."

I kept walking and repeating the words over and over. Praise music filled my spirit through the headset of my Walkman, and the words of the songs mixed with my own words to feed and nourish me. Then, as my eyes took in the soft light glistening off the rolling waves, a tranquil comfort flooded my whole being. All my senses were filled with God's love and the wonder of his creation.

At that moment I noticed a pile of rocks just next to the path that borders the stony shore. A cross made of two sticks was propped up in the middle of the pile, and a rolled-up newspaper was tied to the cross with a ribbon. I unwrapped the paper carefully, not wanting to tear it and fully intending to replace it just as I'd found it. *Someone has taken the time to create this memorial,* I thought, *so I should take the time to consider the message.*

I read the headline across the top of the newspaper, written in bold white numbers on a black background: "9.11.01." Then I noticed the date on the paper: September 11, 2002. Obviously it was the 9/11 anniversary edition. The page was covered with small print, listing the names of all the people killed on September 11, 2001. In the center of the page overlaying the print was the image of a single red rose, and in the center of the rose blossom was the image of an American flag.

I gently hugged the paper and thought, *God has sent me a red rose. This is a love letter from God. God is my husband, and he has sent this gift to me!*

I took the paper home, certain that whoever placed it there wouldn't mind. I wanted it to be a special memento of the first time I thought of the Lord as my husband. In recognition of my new status, I moved my wedding ring from my left hand to my right hand. *God has first claim on my heart,* I thought.

He still does. I am his alone. He is my spiritual husband.

BUT FOR YOU WHO REVERE MY NAME, THE SUN OF
RIGHTEOUSNESS WILL RISE WITH HEALING IN ITS WINGS.

—MALACHI 4:2

LOOKING AT THE PRINCIPLE

GOD USES LIFE'S EXPERIENCES
TO BRING HEALING IN TIME.

1. Life goes on.

No matter what kind of personal tragedy or loss we experience, life does go on. The world continues to rotate on its axis. The sun came up on September 12, 2001, and it has every day since. Slowly people have returned to their normal routines, and healing has taken place. For some who were further removed from the events of 9/11, the pain and loss was relatively minor and the healing was quick. For others of us, the healing continues to this day.

As unfair, unreasonable, and impossible as it seems, we still have work to do after a tragedy occurs. We still have roles to fill. We still have responsibilities to family and others. The stuff of life may pause for a while, but it doesn't stop. Fair or not, that's reality.

And in some ways, reality is not so bad. After a traumatic

loss, picking up the routines of life again—understanding and latching on to what still continues—helps in the healing process. We can find great comfort in seeing what still remains. It reassures us that God is still in control and still on our side.

As healing continues, then, God allows us to assume or re-assume more and more responsibility. He gives comfort, strength, and insight in ways we never imagined. We find our-selves moving from despair to actually looking forward to the future. Our hope is restored; and once again we are glad that life goes on.

2. Healing requires active participation.

After great loss or personal tragedy, the healing process begins almost immediately—if we don't stop the process by refusing to accept God's help. If we remain stuck in our grief, immobilized by pain, the pain will not decrease. It's our choice: We can choose to remain bound up in the grip of our personal suffering, or we can choose to get up and join God in our healing process.

I'll be honest with you: The first few steps of healing hurt terribly. I remember, after giving birth to both of my children, how uncomfortable it was to get up and take *those* first steps. A voice inside me screamed, *No, stay in bed! It hurts too much to move!* Staying in bed and waiting for the pain to go away cer-tainly seemed like the easiest route. But I needed to get up and take those first steps toward healing. The doctor's orders were for my benefit. And ultimately I found that as I worked through those painful first steps, the next steps became easier, and the steps after that easier still.

The same principle applies in times of loss. If we can summon the strength to take the first steps, the healing will come that much sooner. At times I have felt like a child learning to walk for the first time. Thankfully, God has provided people to support me and guide me, both with my first steps as a single parent and my first steps in my new spiritual calling. I have discovered that the more steps I take, the more healing I experience.

If we don't take those first steps and participate with God in our healing process, we die while we are still alive. We've all seen people who have given up. They have no enthusiasm for anything. Life is flat and dull. They stagnate rather than heal, grow, and change. But God doesn't change our feelings so that we can get out of bed and move ahead. He tells us to trust him, get up, and take one more step of faith toward healing—in spite of our feelings.

If you've been incapacitated by pain, begin by telling God that you are ready to take one step forward in your healing process. Prayerfully consider what that one step might be. Remember, you're just taking one step—not running a marathon. Maybe you just need to get up, get dressed, and do one thing today that you haven't been able to do for some time. Take a walk. Call a friend and meet for lunch. Go to the library and pick up a book.

Just don't stay in isolation. Most of us prefer the companionship of others when we are hurting. We might want to be physically alone from time to time, but we don't like feeling abandoned. It is a comfort to know that someone understands our pain and hurts with us. Ultimately that someone is God. He wants to comfort you and heal you, and he wants you to partner with him in that process. As Psalm 34:18 says, "The LORD is close to the brokenhearted and saves those who are crushed in spirit."

When we partner with God, he uses many unique and special means to transform us and bring about healing in our lives. For Jennifer, Tommy, and me, some of our healing came from our participation in the Flag Run across America, an event organized by American and United Airlines pilots. Thousands of people ran and carried the American flag along the same route that American Airlines Flight 11 would have flown from Boston to Los Angeles on that fateful day. We ran the last stretch and crossed the finish line along with many other family members of the crews lost on 9/11. A large crowd welcomed us with cheers and applause as patriotic music played in the background. My kids grinned from ear to ear!

The event was such a celebration of the American spirit. We couldn't help but feel the support of the entire nation at that moment.

Another healing moment occurred when President George W. Bush spoke at the University of New Hampshire. Some friends of ours were involved in the event and got tickets for Jennifer, Tommy, and me. As a bonus we were invited to go to a reception with the president after he spoke.

I felt like a kid! President Bush shook my hand, gave me a fatherly pat on the back and a kiss on the cheek, and then proceeded to give my children some presidential advice: "Listen to your mother." Then he turned to Jennifer's boyfriend and said, "Listen to your girlfriend's mother."

He was so gracious and genuine—just charming! I appreciated his kindness. The meeting was brief, but it was healing nonetheless.

Of course, the ultimate comfort comes from the Lord himself. He is close to us in our suffering and understands how we feel, because he has suffered too. When we comprehend, even slightly, the suffering he endured on our behalf, we can open our hearts to him in gratitude and begin to experience his healing touch.

Since Tom died my heart has known both pain and comfort. But day by day, as the Lord stays close to me, I grow stronger. And the truth of Psalm 147:3 becomes an ever-increasing reality in my life: "He heals the brokenhearted and binds up their wounds."

3. God's provision is sufficient.

Certainly, we don't always feel adequate to fulfill the responsibilities that God has given us. So often our frailties seem to overshadow our strengths, and we fear that we won't be able to move past our difficulties and succeed in our calling.

But God is the one who calls us, and he is the one who equips us. It is his desire that his work be accomplished, and it's his responsibility to make sure we're up to the task. He doesn't set us up to fail; he makes provision for us. Whatever we need, whatever the resource, he will provide it at just the right time so that we can do his work.

Philippians 4:19 says, "And my God will meet all your needs according to his glorious riches in Christ Jesus." That provision may not always come in ways that we expect. But when we do what we can with what we have and trust God for the rest, he provides.

Soon after 9/11 I realized that I needed large doses of strength and courage to handle all the details of our new life. I believed that God would provide for our needs, but I also knew that I had to act on our behalf to take hold of that provision.

One of the more difficult decisions I faced was whether or not to take advantage of the federal government's September 11th Victim Compensation Fund. Controversy swirled: Why should people who lost loved ones in the World Trade Center disaster receive financial help when victims of other tragedies, such as the 1995 bombing in Oklahoma City, did not? Why should one family be eligible to receive one amount while another family is eligible to receive a different amount? Is one life worth more than another life? What about the potential for future lawsuits? There were no easy answers.

I agonized and prayed and agonized again. Then God granted me peace. I came to the conclusion that the money wasn't compensation for Tom's life. You can't place a dollar amount on a human life! Rather, the financial benefits from the Victim Compensation Fund were part of God's plan for providing for us. They were his provision, allowing us to move forward to do his will and accomplish his work. God didn't plant a money tree in the backyard, but he did use the compassion of lawmakers to provide this resource.

Once the decision was made, I had to face the application process. This included many meetings with attorneys and CPAs—and I'd been out of the "power suit" world for some time. It was all a bit daunting.

The strength and courage I needed to go into those meetings

and effectively represent myself and my children required supernatural means. I needed the Holy Spirit to lead me as I dealt with issues that appeared to be practical but had ethical and spiritual implications. I needed the wisdom of God's Word to deal with questions that had no one right or wrong answer.

Each day I would go into the family room early in the morning before the children got up and sit down with my Bible. I'd pray, looking out the window at the trees and sunlight and clouds. I'd breathe deeply—breathe in the goodness of God and breathe out my anxiety. I'd read Psalms and ask God to settle my heart. Invariably, through this daily quiet time with the Lord, I would receive the strength I needed, not only for deciding legal matters but for making other decisions as well.

I continue this process to this day. I begin each day with God, pray all day long, and trust that he will meet my every need.

4. Many details about the future remain unknown.

Walking with Jesus involves walking by faith. Our attempts to control the future are fruitless. Those of us who have suffered loss understand only too well that we control very little in our lives.

The promise of tomorrow is given to no one. We need to appreciate each day as a special gift from God and focus our hearts on him, seeking to know and understand his will on a day-by-day basis. We need to take God's Word to heart when he tells us in Matthew 6:34, "Therefore do not worry about tomorrow, for tomorrow will worry about itself. Each day has enough trouble of its own."

When we let go of the false belief that we are in control of our lives, we give God room to come in and comfort us with the knowledge that he, our loving heavenly Father, is in control. Acknowledging that God is in control doesn't mean that our lives will be pain free. It does mean we will worry and fret less over things we can't change and pay more attention to those things we can change.

Even with an unknown future, we have cause for great hope. God is our partner in life. We can trust that he will be with us, no matter what. He will rejoice with us in the good times and walk next to us—sometimes even carry us—through the painful times. However broken or devastated we feel, his transforming power will lift us up and restore wholeness.

I never believed I could survive without Tom. But I am surviving. And so will you. You may be at a place of despair. You may see no way to overcome your fears. But in time and with God's healing, you will be able to live well again—if you put your faith and trust in Jesus. As a Christian you can have hope for the future. Because God walks with you. And heaven lies ahead of you.

At that moment I realized I needed to forgive the evil of 9/11 and the personal pain it caused me. I had to make a choice: to hold on to hatred or to forgive.

Chapter Eleven

GOD AT GROUND ZERO

Principle 11

GOD CALLS YOU TO HAVE AN ETERNAL PERSPECTIVE.

Looking up at the buildings of New York City, I felt as if I were walking on an alien planet. I moved along with the crowds, wondering, *Which direction did Tom's plane come from? How low was it flying? What did he see as the nightmare unfolded? The people around me now—the ones who live and work on this busy street—were they here on that fateful day?* My mind raced back to a romantic weekend Tom and I had shared in New York years before. It was difficult to grasp all that had happened in the city and in my life since that idyllic time.

I'd had many invitations to go to New York City since 9/11,

but I'd turned them all down. I just wasn't ready. Then a meeting was scheduled for surviving family members who wanted to participate in the Victim Compensation Fund. The date was July 8, 2002, ten months after the tragedy. It seemed that my decision about if and when to go to New York had been made for me.

A few days prior to my trip, I began to feel apprehensive. Jennifer was the one who gave me the strength to follow through with my plans. She reminded me of the analogy Tom used to illustrate the body and soul being like a hand in a glove. When we die, Tom would say, our body goes into the ground, while our soul goes to heaven. Jennifer encouraged me to go to Ground Zero but to remember that Tom was not there. How wonderful it was to hear such wisdom from my daughter, knowing that she shared the same loss!

And so I went to New York. I took the train; I didn't want to fly the same route that Tom had flown on September 11. I attended the Victim Compensation Fund meeting, then set my sights on Ground Zero.

Steamy heat rose from the sidewalk, trapped in the breezeless canyon between highrises. I flagged a cab and asked the driver to take me to the site of the World Trade Center. He grunted a response. *My husband was the copilot on the first plane that hit the towers on September 11*, I said silently to the back of the driver's head. Why would he care? He'd probably driven hundreds of people to the site. Maybe he lost someone he loved that day too.

I leaned back against the cool seat and closed my eyes. My emotions choked my throat as I tried to grasp what I was doing. It was right here, right in this city, right on this street and the streets adjacent to it, that life changed forever for me, my children, and for so many others.

When I opened my eyes again, I saw that the cab had entered an area full of construction-site signs and roadblocks. Apparently taxicabs were allowed to take passengers between the barriers and drop them off very close to Ground Zero. I stepped out of the cab and into a scene that chilled every nerve in my body. A tall chain-link fence stretched for blocks to my left and right. I'd seen the pictures on television of this makeshift memorial, but to view it up close magnified the horror of so many lives lost. Photos, notes, flowers dried by their lengthy vigil, baseball caps, T-shirts: All hung on the fence or rested at its base, representing so many grieving hearts left behind. I just stood and looked, unable to move for some time.

Eventually I began walking in the direction I thought would take me to the actual spot where the World Trade Center once stood. I turned one corner and then another, following the people around me. They were not so much a crowd as a silent group of mourners. Finally we walked through a tunnel and came out in front of a deep pit. Ground Zero. The place where Tom's plane had disappeared into the rubble.

What Happened?

Many people have tried to speculate about what happened inside Tom's plane that morning of 9/11. I never wanted to know all the gruesome details. Apparently the passengers on Tom's flight didn't have the opportunity to make cell phone calls, as passengers on the other doomed flights did; so many of the specific details will never be known. I do know that Tom would have been doing whatever he could have done to get the aircraft safely on the ground. He would have been thinking about the welfare of the passengers and about Jennifer, Tommy, and me. He never would have flown the plane into the World Trade Center, so I'm certain he wasn't at the controls when it hit. Was he being restrained or perhaps sitting by a passenger or—? I don't know.

In the early months after 9/11, I asked a few pilots what they thought might have happened inside the plane, but they were hesitant to say. I appreciated their sensitivity. I found that whenever my mind would veer off in a gruesome direction, my spirit would hit rock bottom and crash. I simply couldn't go there. I chose to let what actually happened remain unknown to me. I could almost hear God saying, *Cheryl, don't look that way. Look at me. This is where Tom is. I have him. He is in my arms.*

What gave my heart rest—what still gives it rest—is the assurance I have that whatever happened, Tom was quickly ushered from this world into the arms of Jesus and up to heaven. It's as if God wrapped a protective bubble around me that to this day keeps the horror of what happened out, and the assurance of his love in. Tom is safe with Jesus in heaven, and I am safe with Jesus here on earth.

Moving toward Forgiveness

That day in July, standing on the platform at Ground Zero, my emotions were overwhelmed. I was speechless. How could words adequately describe the magnitude of the destruction that had been rendered upon so many by the actions of a few? The familiar television-screen images of the hijackers' faces hung like a gossamer shroud over the pit. *This place is the result of evil,* I thought. *Terrible, terrible evil.*

The events of that day were not a crime against the United States. The acts of those nineteen individuals on September 11, 2001, were not an attack of Muslims against Christians or even nation against nation. No, it was a crime against all humanity, representing the worst that mankind has to offer— man's inhumanity directed toward man in a most horrendous

223

way. It was a senseless demonstration of the depravity of human beings, a sad and sorrowful picture of the worst we are capable of as a species.

I looked down into the dull gray pit, where traces of the cleanup were still visible in piles of cement rubble and wires sticking out of the ground. Light, intermittent breezes ruffled the dirt and stirred up little swirls of dust. The sounds of the city buzzed in the background, but the edges of the pit screamed with the silence of devastation.

As I looked from one side of the massive expanse to the other, my eyes fixed on the only steel structure left standing. It was in the shape of a cross. I kept turning my head back and forth, first to the pit and then to the cross. Then I stopped looking at the pit and stayed focused on the cross.

How can you forgive what man has done? I cried out to God in my heart. *How can you forgive this evil devastation and destruction?*

Then suddenly I felt as if I were at the base of the cross of Christ, on my knees in the dust, guilty of my own offenses against God and others, with God's voice speaking to me: "I forgive you, Cheryl." *God knows the full extent of the evil committed on 9/11,* I thought, *because that evil was done to him as well.* I pictured Jesus hanging on the cross, nails piercing his hands and feet, a crown of thorns on his head. The rebellion of man put him there. Not only the men involved in the hijackings. But all of us. *I put him there.*

At that moment I was filled with such gratitude for what Jesus did on the cross—and for the reality that because of his sacrifice, Tom and I will be reunited in heaven one day—that I determined to spend the rest of my days serving the Lord. And I realized that part of that service would involve telling others how good God is and how much he loves us. How he gives us what we need and restores our brokenness. How in the midst of the inevitable pain of life, he supernaturally comes into our hearts and heals us.

At that moment I also realized I needed to forgive the evil of 9/11 and the personal pain it caused me. I had to make a choice: to hold on to hatred or to forgive. To focus on the pit of evil and destruction, or to focus on the cross of Christ.

I chose to forgive.

After I left New York City, I began to feel more and more that God wanted me to speak publicly about forgiveness. I wasn't sure what to do with this feeling, but I couldn't shake it. It was as if God were whispering deep in my spirit, "Cheryl, you are my messenger, and I want you to share these thoughts with others." As the weeks went by, he made it clearer and clearer to me that this was, indeed, his call on my life. But how was I going to follow through on this calling? What exactly was I going to say?

As I was sorting through some of Tom's books one day, I came across one of his study guides. In it were some notes—very compelling notes—that he'd written about forgiveness. I found myself reading: "Father, forgive them, for they do not know what they are doing." "Love your enemies and pray for those who persecute you." "Be merciful just as your Father is merciful." "Be kind and compassionate to one another, forgiving each other just as in Christ God forgave you."

Tom was paraphrasing God's Word, but there was no mistaking his handwriting. The thought came to me: *He is asking us to forgive those who hurt him.* Looking down at that one key word written in Tom's own hand, I could almost hear him saying it: "Forgive."

But how could I forgive? It seemed so unreasonable! How could I forgive the men who planned and carried out the attack on the towers? How could I let go of the thought of vengeance, of hurting those who hurt the man I treasured more than life? The very idea seemed so unfair.

Then I asked myself, *Did Tom really mean these words that he wrote?* Before I even finished the question, I knew the answer: Yes, he did. Tom was a man who lived his faith. I couldn't ignore that aspect of his legacy. If I proclaimed myself to be a woman of

God, I had to work toward forgiveness. It was not optional; it was essential.

The more I considered this idea of forgiveness, the more confident I became that in Christ I would be able to forgive what seemed to be unforgivable. I realized that we all choose what we dwell on. And what we dwell on determines in large measure our attitudes. I knew that if I dwelt on anger, I would become resentful. If I stayed resentful, I would become bitter. If I stayed bitter, my heart wouldn't fully heal. And I wanted my heart to be healed! So I resolved that I would not let the terrorists win the war for my heart. And I would do everything I could to keep them from winning the war for my children's hearts.

I asked God to work the miracle of forgiveness in my heart. I knew that I needed to model for Jennifer and Tommy an attitude toward others that included forgiveness. By my example I needed to encourage them to demonstrate God's love in the midst of an evil world.

And so here I am today, learning to forgive. I can't do it in my own strength. But I'm discovering that as I allow God's love to fill my heart, the power of his Holy Spirit helps me to see the beauty beyond the ashes. The faces of the hijackers disappear into the mist above the site of the World Trade Center, and the empty cross rises up. And I see Tom being carried home, cradled in the arms of Jesus.

OBEY ME, AND I WILL BE YOUR GOD AND YOU WILL BE
MY PEOPLE. WALK IN ALL THE WAYS I COMMAND YOU,
THAT IT MAY GO WELL WITH YOU.

—JEREMIAH 7:23

LOOKING AT THE PRINCIPLE

GOD CALLS YOU TO HAVE AN ETERNAL PERSPECTIVE.

1. The things of this world are temporary.

Whatever we construct in this life, whatever physical symbols
of success we may create, can disappear in a heartbeat. Whether
it is the twin towers of the World Trade Center or some other
tangible evidence of accomplishment, we know from God's
Word that it will ultimately be rendered worthless—just so
much hay and stubble.

As Christians we need to direct our time, energy, and focus
toward those things that are permanent, those things that will
produce an eternal result. What we do to create stronger relationships with those we love, for example, is so much more
important than what we do to accumulate things. We need to
be constantly developing our spiritual dimension and drawing
closer to God. And we need to do all we can to create legacies
that will draw others to him.

2. With God an eternal perspective is paramount.

Jesus says in Matthew 10:28–31, "Do not be afraid of those who kill the body but cannot kill the soul. Rather, be afraid of the One who can destroy both soul and body in hell. Are not two sparrows sold for a penny? Yet not one of them will fall to the ground apart from the will of your Father. And even the very hairs on your head are all numbered. So don't be afraid; you are worth more than many sparrows."

Many of us fear death. We're scared of the possibility of physical pain, frightened by the prospect of the experience of death. But according to God's Word, the death of the soul, not the death of the body, is the thing we should be concerned about. The body is not meant to live forever. The soul is designed for eternity.

For most of us, the concept of eternity is beyond our ability to grasp. Tommy likes to share a lesson his dad taught him about eternity. He remembers Tom telling him, "If you took all the oceans of the world and removed the water one drop at a time, when you were finished, you would only have experienced the beginning of eternity." What a picture! Eternity runs on with no beginning and no end. It is infinite. Whatever our allotted number of years of life on earth, it is no comparison against the measure of all eternity. From an eternal perspective, our life here is like the blink of an eye.

Yes, it is painful to think that Tom's life on earth was cut short by possibly thirty, forty, fifty years or more. From an earthly perspective, it seems so unfair. But I take enormous comfort in knowing that Tom's life did not end. He simply moved ahead to begin his time with our Lord for eternity.

God calls us to have an eternal perspective. That eternal perspective should permeate all of our thoughts, words, and deeds. It should be foremost in all of our relationships—our relationships with others here in this life and our relationship with the Lord.

3. Forgiveness is not optional.

God's Word is very clear. In Luke 6:37 Jesus instructs us, "Do not judge, and you will not be judged. Do not condemn, and you will not be condemned. Forgive, and you will be forgiven."

Jesus' own example is compelling. He even prayed for his executioners from the cross, "Father, forgive them, for they do not know what they are doing" (Luke 23:34). We are called to follow that example—to forgive one another just as Christ has forgiven us. To be merciful to others just as God is merciful to us. Forgiveness is not optional; it's essential for life in Christ.

4. True forgiveness comes from God.

Forgiveness doesn't come naturally. On our own we are simply unable to forgive the injustices inflicted upon us. But with God all things are possible. God is the author of forgiveness, and his most gracious demonstration of that fact is the giving of his Son on our behalf. We turned from him, and yet he provided a way for us to be reconciled to him. When we forgive, make no mistake: It is the power of God at work in us that enables us to do so.

To forgive we must let go of anger and bitterness. Of course, anger is often a natural part of the grief process. But if we harbor that anger, it will destroy us. Anger soon turns to bitterness, and bitterness renders the heart hard and unloving. We become like those who have hurt us.

Letting go of anger and bitterness begins when we ask God to turn our thoughts to him and away from evil. By setting our minds on his great love instead of on the cause of our pain, our hearts overflow with gratitude that God's grace came to us when we needed it most. We begin to comprehend what it means to be forgiven. We see our own sins—sins that make us guilty in ways perhaps not so obvious as those of the 9/11 hijackers, but sins nonetheless. Yet God loved us enough to send his Son to pay the penalty for those sins! When we understand that, forgiving others becomes so much easier.

Sometimes we can't offer forgiveness directly. Certainly in the case of 9/11, we can't go to the men who perpetrated the hijackings and say, "I forgive you." But we can offer our forgiveness back to God. We can go to God and say, "I forgive them, Lord." And we can ask God to forgive them, just as Jesus did when he hung on the cross and asked God to forgive his offenders.

God's forgiveness of the hijackers doesn't mean they will go unpunished for their deeds. God is a righteous judge. Rather, it means that we are no longer saddled with the heavy weight of unforgiveness in our lives. We are free from the burden of carrying a judgment that is not ours to render. That judgment belongs to God alone.

My prayer is that you will also come to know hope, not despair; courage, not fear; love, not hate.

Chapter Twelve

HOPE FOR TOMORROW

Principle 12

GOD HAS A PLAN FOR THE REST OF YOUR LIFE.

A very dear friend once asked me to imagine this scene:

I am at home with Tom on September 10, 2001—the day before the terrible tragedy of 9/11—and as I look out my front window, I see Jesus walking up my driveway. He comes to the door and knocks. Tom and I eagerly throw open the door and welcome him into our home.

He sits down in our living room and, after a little general conversation, says to us, "I have something very important to tell you. I want you to listen very carefully to what I'm about to say."

Jesus goes on to tell us that a horrible tragedy is about to take place the next day. Thousands of people will be killed. The event will tear the hearts out of many thousands more. People will be shocked, scared, and dazed. Lives will be shattered, and the pain will be felt around the world.

"But," Jesus says, "I will use this tragedy, this disaster, to reach many thousands more for the kingdom of God. In fact, I will use both of you in very special ways as part of my plan. I will use you to touch many lives. Cheryl, you will share the words I will put on your heart, so that others might find hope in the face of trials and rise above their circumstances, whatever they are."

Then he adds, "I need Tom to be part of my work too. You see, tomorrow I will call Tom home to be with me. Tom's death, along with the deaths of thousands more, will result in many coming to know me. And many more will have their lives changed, their faith deepened, and their love for me and others increased—all because of your sacrifice."

I sit there in shock and disbelief. "No, Lord. No!" I scream. "I'm not ready to let Tom go. Please don't take him."

Jesus knows my anguish. He reaches over and touches me. He takes my hand and Tom's, and he prays with us. He prays for us. He holds us. And he weeps with us. He says, "I know it's hard—but trust me."

On September 11, 2001, the day my nightmare began, I knew God, but I didn't have the ability to trust him completely. I loved him, but I couldn't bring myself to turn over every aspect of my life to him. In the months that followed, however, God slowly turned my disbelief into belief. I have learned that God is my refuge and my strength. I have learned that he does truly love me. And I have come to see that I can trust him in all things. I couldn't see that on September 11—not like I see it today. But over these passing months and now years, my Prince of Peace has brought me peace and given me hope.

Before September 11, I never could have imagined the pain and devastation that lay ahead for me and my family. But then the unimaginable happened. Thankfully, on that day, God was holding us in his hands. And he never let go. He carried all four of us—Tom, Jennifer, Tommy, and me—through the horror of 9/11. He taught us the truth of Romans 5:3–5: "Not only so, but we also rejoice in our sufferings, because we know that suffering produces perseverance; perseverance, character; and character, hope. And hope does not disappoint us, because God has poured out his love into our hearts by the Holy Spirit, whom he has given us."

God showed us that we could place our hope and trust in him. He showed us that in him, we could find the strength to overcome any life circumstance.

My prayer is that you, by God's grace and power, will also come to know hope, not despair; courage, not fear; love, not hate. Yes, we all experience pain, suffering, and loss at some point in our lives. Yes, there are challenges ahead for each of us. But through those challenges, God will find ways to show us he still loves us and cares for us. He will find ways to make his presence known and to help us through. As believers we have that hope.

I have that hope.

I LOVE YOU, O LORD, MY STRENGTH. THE LORD IS MY ROCK, MY FORTRESS AND MY DELIVERER; MY GOD IS MY ROCK, IN WHOM I TAKE REFUGE. HE IS MY SHIELD AND THE HORN OF MY SALVATION, MY STRONGHOLD. I CALL TO THE LORD, WHO IS WORTHY OF PRAISE, AND I AM SAVED FROM MY ENEMIES.

—PSALM 18:1–3

LOOKING AT THE PRINCIPLE

GOD HAS A PLAN FOR THE REST OF YOUR LIFE.

1. You and I matter to God.

You've read my story now and have seen how God has worked, and continues to work, in my life. The backdrop for my story is September 11, 2001—a uniquely horrific day that riveted the attention of the entire world. But had Tom not been on that particular plane on that particular morning, my story would probably be a lot like yours: a simple person, a typical family, seeking to serve God and walk with him day by day, never making headline news.

Sometimes we're tempted to think that our individual lives don't count for much in God's economy—that what we do doesn't matter as much as what the next person does. Nothing could be further from the truth. Each of us is important and valuable in God's eyes. Each of us has a contribution to make to the work of his kingdom here on earth. What we do depends on our unique gifts and talents and the opportunities he gives us. But each of us has an important role to play.

God has opened the door for me to speak and write about his love and forgiveness. He has opened different doors for you. He cares about your life as much as he does about mine. He loves you and wants you to know him intimately. He wants to use you—uniquely you—for the furtherance of his kingdom.

We need to let go of comparisons. When we stop comparing ourselves to each other, we find that we can give and serve in ways that reflect who we are in Christ. We can step out of our comfort zones, do things we never believed possible, and receive fulfillment from even the most unnoticed acts of service. For example, maybe you are called to be an encourager to others, to talk with and listen to people in pain. At the end of the day, you may not have hours clocked in or a time sheet that shows how much you worked; but you can know in your spirit that your work for God's kingdom was truly valuable.

Here's the bottom line: We matter a great deal to God. This statement seems so evident, but many of us don't live as if we believe it. We've grown so accustomed to the words of the gospel, *Jesus died for my sins*, that they no longer have the power to affect our spirits. We need to open our hearts and believe! If we will do that, we'll find ourselves growing more and more excited about what God has in store for the rest of our lives.

2. Focus on the feast.

God has prepared a banquet table for us. He has invited us to sit at his table and enjoy to our hearts content all that he has for us. He has piled the table high with every imaginable blessing. And he has promised to continue to put more and more blessings on the table for us to feast upon.

But where are we? What are we focused on? More often than not, our focus is not on the feast on the table; it is on the stuff that is not there. We focus on what we want but don't have. We focus on what we want rather than what he is offering us.

It happens all the time. It is a very natural reaction to loss. Even when we are not struggling with loss, even when things are going great, we still do it. I don't know why. It just seems like we are wired to think that way.

For me it is easy to slip into moments of despair, to struggle with all that I don't have because of September 11—my husband is gone, my children's father is gone, our dream is gone, and the list goes on. And while I sit at the table and survey the feast the Lord has provided, as I see right in front of me the richness of his love, I still find myself looking over to the side and saying, "But Lord, what I want isn't on this table, it is over there. That is what I want." And God, my loving father says to me, "Why are you looking over there when I have given you all this to enjoy? Why are you focused on what you don't have instead of all that I have for you?"

The solution I have found lies in conforming my will to his. The more I focus on him, the more I am able to see that his offering is so much more than my own desires. The more we can, as Paul wrote in Romans 12, be transformed by the renewing of our minds, we will be able to test and approve what God's will is—his good, pleasing, and perfect will. Or as Tom once said to Jennifer, "If you want to have everything you want, just want everything you have."

The secret is to keep focus on the feast—to celebrate all that he has given to us—and to know that he is preparing more blessings for tomorrow. He loves us that much.

3. God wants us to meet with him regularly to share our hearts.

If we have really embraced God's love for us and the belief that he has a plan for us, we will be eager to meet with him, pour out our hearts, and wait quietly for his whisper. Our regular times with the Lord will be a blessing of refreshment, revealing to us the day-to-day unfolding of God's direction in our lives. We must never allow the busyness of life to rob us of the quiet times that fill our souls with God's goodness!

4. Not all questions in life get answered.

Maybe you feel that the plan for your life is littered with question marks. You don't understand why you are where you are or why you're having to struggle with a particular circumstance.

I understand. There are so many of life's difficult questions that remain unanswered for me. I don't know why the events of 9/11 occurred. I don't know why God didn't intervene. I don't know why innocent people suffered then and continue to suffer now in so many ways.

Of course, the pat theological answer is that we live in a sinful world. Sin happens; therefore suffering happens, even to innocents. But God doesn't give pat answers to difficult questions. I believe that his purposes are greater than we can begin to comprehend, and the answers to our questions are often far beyond our ability to understand.

God may not always explain things the way we want him to. But in his goodness, he reveals to each of us exactly what we need to live obediently as his children and to make choices consistent with his teachings in Scripture. We free ourselves to live as he wants us to live when we lay down the need for answers to all of our questions. If we don't give up our demand for answers, however, our days become haunted by the deafening silence we get in response to questions we're not meant to understand.

The key is to stop asking, why did this happen? and start asking, what does God want me to do in this situation? Remember, God is infinitely wiser than we are. He knows what is best for us. Like children trusting a loving parent, we are able to move forward in life only as we trust God, acknowledge our dependence on him, and take one step at a time toward him.

We don't have to understand everything. We don't have to know in advance every step of the plan he has for us. We merely have to fall into the loving arms of his embrace and say, "Father, help me."

And he will.

In the months that followed September 11, 2001, God slowly turned my fear into courage, my uncertainty into confidence, and my pain and suffering into peace and contentment.

I know now that I can trust God in all things.

You can too.

And for that I will always be thankful.

If you want to further explore the principles and concepts shared in this book, go to www.beautybeyondtheashes.com for a set of thought-provoking questions that are ideal for group discussion or personal reflection.

The Ministry of
Cheryl McGuinness
BEAUTY BEYOND THE ASHES

Rising from the Ashes . . .

Cheryl McGuinness is a woman with a story . . . a story of tragedy, immeasurable pain, forgiveness, hope, healing, and ultimately, peace.

Her world changed in a heartbeat on September 11, 2001. Her husband, Tom McGuinness, was copilot of American Airlines Flight 11, which slammed into the World Trade Center that fateful morning.

Although the pain visits her on a daily basis, Cheryl's faith in a loving and sovereign God has provided the strength to rise above her circumstances, to parent her two teenaged children, and to begin life anew.

Nationally recognized, sought-after speaker Cheryl McGuinness has a passion for helping those who live with heartbreak. Her presentations offer hope and encouragement to the wounded.

For More Information

To schedule a speaking engagement with Cheryl, e-mail Deb at Debw@tobystowe.com, call Deb at 603.433.8838, or visit Cheryl's Web site at www.beautybeyondtheashes.com for upcoming engagements.

Beauty Beyond the Ashes
PO Box 6616
Portsmouth, NH 03802-6616

HE HAS SENT ME TO BIND UP THE BROKENHEARTED, . . .
TO BESTOW ON THEM A CROWN OF BEAUTY INSTEAD OF ASHES.
—ISAIAH 61:1, 3

What Others Are Saying about Cheryl's Ministry . . .

"God has done amazing things through all of this. Thank you for giving us so much of yourself to help the rest of the world heal. Your strength and trust is such an inspiration."

"God is surely with you to allow you to speak to such a large crowd so eloquently."

"You are such an inspiration to me personally in my spiritual walk that I can't get you out of my head. Your strength and faith in our Lord is an example that I feel we all need to see."

"Your talk and testimony felt so strong—I was amazed at your strength. Thank you for sharing such grace and courage, for giving us the most powerful feeling of God's love, for allowing us to share your pain, and for so much more. You are a huge example of how God works."

"Thank you so much for blessing those of us who heard you speak about your blessings as we gathered in the Italian Community Center in Milwaukee today. The hand of God on your life was apparent to me and all of us who were touched by your gentle words."